MODERN AMERICAN WRITERS

VIII. WILLA CATHER

MODERN AMERICAN WRITERS

Edited by ERNEST BOYD

WILLA CATHER

By

RENÉ RAPIN

ROBERT M. McBRIDE & COMPANY
NEW YORK   ::   ::   ::   MCMXXX

WILLA CATHER

I

CONTEMPORARY criticism lacks perspective. There is no better proof of this than the welcome given to a new book by a writer already famous. Whatever its worth, whatever its girth, it is always So-and-so's latest masterpiece. There is sometimes an attempt to appraise it in the light of the author's former work, but too often the reader is hard put to it to see if the reviewer is praising another *Tess of the D'Urbervilles* or a work—perfectly charming perhaps, not to be easily matched among its own diminutive peers—of the third or fourth magnitude. The reviewer may damn with faint praise: the book must be very bad indeed for him to dare to say Mr. Famous Writer's latest is bad.

Willa Cather has never published a bad book. Ergo, all of her work is of the same excellence, all of it has the same importance: thus, at least do too many critics and reviewers seem to argue. If they venture to praise one book above the others, even the best must needs choose—a typical example of the lack of perspective—a novelette like *A Lost Lady*. I am not insensitive to *A Lost Lady's* charm. It has some of Willa Cather's finest touches, it has delicacy, it has pathos. I am even willing to call it a perfect full-length portrait—on a small scale. But why call it her best work when she has written *One of Ours*, *The Professor's House*, *Death Comes for the Archbishop*, works of sustained power, breadth of vision and of compass, variety of interest, truly to be called great? Also (shall I confess it, when no critic that I have read has

1

admitted as much?), if few books are more fascinating than Willa Cather's, few are more disappointing sometimes. Take some of her best, *O Pioneers*, *My Ántonia*, *The Song of the Lark*—some would add *The Professor's House*; I do not—the first one hundred, two hundred, three hundred pages even (as in *The Song of the Lark*) read like magic. A world whose existence, whose beauty you did not suspect opens to you, silently unfolds around you, stretches out in front of you, rich in incident and in promise. You feel the strong impact of the Nebraskan wind, your very breathing comes deep and passionate like Thea Kronborg's or My Ántonia's. Then the unexpected happens: the tension drops, the tempo suddenly slows, there is a slackening of the sails, a shifting of the center of interest. You were following Thea Kronborg's dogged fight with a world which seems not to want art unless it be the cheap sentimental, you were battling with her against poverty, and the merciless demands of the most exacting of callings. You are asked now to indulge in a peaceful interlude *à deux*, deep in an enchanted canyon, and, once that beautiful, unheroic episode is over—its beauty other-worldly and carefree like that of Keats's *Grecian Urn*—it is, alas, but glimpses of Thea's real self, her fighting self, that Willa Cather allows you.

I do not grudge Willa Cather the episode (there is a similar one in *The Professor's House* which I am ready to defend against all comers); I grudge her the sudden fall of tension, the more so as it is never recovered afterwards. More disappointing, as the break occurs after but seventy pages in the one book, one hundred and sixty in the other, the similar "accidents" in *O Pioneers* and *My Ántonia*. You were sharing the Bergsons' or the Shimerdas' pioneer existence, their joys and pains, their hardy struggle in the wild new country; and down comes the curtain. When it rises again, three years (*My Ántonia*), sixteen years (*O Pioneers*) have passed. Gone is the endless stretch of the red grass, gone are the hardships of pioneer days, the Shimerdas' primitive dug-out, the Bergsons' low log-house on the ridge; gone Russian Peter and Pavel. Square fields of wheat and corn have replaced the prairie; Alexandra is Alexandra yet, and, if the heroic days are no more, there is still passion, Emil and Marie's tragic love. But where is *our* Ántonia? Ántonia has gone to town, she is like any small town girl now, almost. Lost is her epic grandeur when she stood magnified against the sunset, with infinitude around her. . . .

Willa Cather's work is unfinished as yet. Rash would it be to prophesy whither its curve will be tending now; too early to give either a complete biographical sketch of the author or a final appreciation of her work. My attempt, after a rapid first glance at the stage and the characters, will be to bring what we happen to know of Willa Cather's life to bear upon her work; to take her books in the order they were written, trying to estimate what Willa Cather set out to accomplish and what she has achieved, examining each book in itself and in relation with at least its immediate predecessor, giving an idea of its relative importance (sometimes only by the greater or smaller space assigned to it), concluding with a tentative drawing of the curve that goes from her first stories and poems to her latest novel, summing up at last what peculiarly "Willa Cather qualities" we have observed in the course of this short survey.

Willa Cather would probably be a writer even had she never gone West in her early impressionable years. What kind of a writer, it would be hard to say. Some presumption there is however (the inferior quality of her non-Western books) that we should not have had anything like her present masterpieces, and that America and the world would not have heard of her.

Willa Cather's is indeed a case of the mystic alliance between poet and landscape where each gives to each, the poet giving his chosen country (and the people who live on it and of it, mold it to their image and are molded by it) expression and duration forever, the country and the people so identifying themselves with the poet as to become backbone and marrow of his work. Such Thomas Hardy's union with Wessex, C. F. Ramuz' with Vaud and Valais, Willa Cather's with the great table-lands east of the Rockies. Hardy's sympathies were with the Wessex rustics and with their best sons, the Jude who tries to rise from them to a higher life, the Clym Yeobright who gladly gives up the world for austere Egdon Heath; Ramuz' are with the fishermen, *vignerons*, mountaineers, the poor simple souls who, having little or nothing, have not lost contact with the immediate realities and, being untrammeled, unadulterated by the schooling and conventions of bourgeois society, are capable of imagination and passion and of living original lives. Even so does Willa Cather take to her heart the simplest souls of the West, the generous, impulsive, loyal souls of brakeman, ranchman, pioneer, missionary priest and Indian. As Hardy has his Jude and his Clym Yeobright, Ramuz his Aimé Pache or his Samuel Belet, born of the soil, strong of its strength, yet infinitely above their peasant brothers by their sensitiveness, the intensity of their imagination and their superior consciousness, Willa Cather has her Thea Kronborg, her Claude Wheeler, her Tom Outland, her Professor St. Peter, her Archbishop (though not peasant-born he), carrying the pioneers' flag of endurance into the higher realms, driven on by their imagination and their passion to a more perfect gift of themselves.

But it is not only the West of to-day or of pioneer days that Willa Cather thus expresses and loves. Her heart's warm embrace, the life-giving touch of her art, extend through the years that they abolish to the Indian Cliff Dwellers' first pathetic attempt to secure, in the very midst of insecurity, dignity, social life, art, a humane culture.

Book after book her conquest extended, south being the main trend of her march, Mexico-wards, Indian-wards:

1913—*O Pioneers*, Nebraska of the '80's and the '90's;

1915—*The Song of the Lark*, contemporary Colorado, Chicago, a north Arizona Cliff Dweller canyon;

1918—*My Ántonia*, the Nebraska of *O Pioneers* again;

1922—*One of Ours*, contemporary Nebraska;

1923—*A Lost Lady*, somewhere on the Burlington Route, halfway between Omaha and Denver; time: "the very end of the road-making West";

1925—*The Professor's House*, Michigan, the Cliff Dwellers (New Mexico) again;

1927—*Death Comes for the Archbishop*, New Mexico in the '50's, with excursions back to the Spanish Conquest and allusions to the Cliff Dwellers once more.

Cliff Dwellers, Spanish Conquerors, French, Bohemian, Norwegian pioneers, modern American farmers, railroad men and professors, a motley assemblage, yet *one* at heart, united as they are by their dreams and by the unchanging West.

Willa Cather's West! A country of contrasts: snowed-in winters, "breathless brilliant" summers[1]; plains endless, monotonous, with hardly a swell of the ground; equally monotonous sand-hills; the sudden gap of a canyon, like a gash in a stolid face; model farms and ranches, reapers, binders, threshers, Main Streets, Round Houses, Methodist Churches, like any in any of the States; opals, gold, pockets of virgin silver, geometrical patterns on the clay vessels of an extinct, unmechanical civilization; caustic farmers from New England, lively, gesticulating boys of Gallic or Slavonic blood, blond Scandinavians side by side with dark Bohemians; Mexicans in black velvet;

gallant brakemen, erratic German musicians, songs in "Mexican Town."

A breath of adventure or beauty fans the embers in hearts (the farmer's, the railroad man's, the professor's, the doctor's) depressed by mechanical chores, dulled by a life enslaved to material ends and a dry dead conformity. Mile after mile of red grass, sagebrush, cornfields, sand-hills, bathed in glittering sunlight, deep-buried under snow, blizzard-swept, starred-upon—and lo, at the horizon, a quadruple range of gigantic presences, the airy towers and white shining spires of the Mountains!

II

NASCITUR poeta, non fit. The ancient tag, like most proverbs, is Janus-faced—truth or palpable falsity according to which side you look at. No man not a poet will make himself one: true, but is poetry ever *given* to the poet? The mystic union of artist and landscape seldom comes of itself. When it does—as apparently happened to Willa Cather, more fortunate in this than either Hardy or Ramuz—all is not achieved: the artist has still to conquer himself and his art. He must realize his originality, save what is most precious in him from the avid grasp of the world, the temptations of distraction, passive enjoyment, destructive self-analysis, the flattery of incompetent or biased praise, the indifference or the sneers of men; he must wrestle with himself, oblige himself to dare to say what he feels, to dare to show what he sees *as he sees it*, rewarded at last if he but attain, after how many disappointments, a form not too unworthy of his tremendous hopes, strong enough to bear, subtle and musical enough to sing, his exultations and his agonies.

If Willa Cather's early transplantation to the West brought about for her, without her striving for it, that revelation of a landscape's essential beauty and of the particular imprint on it of human sufferings and toil which comes to other artists after years of groping and exile, her Destiny did not spare her the long painful struggle for originality and a form. Of the process of the struggle we know very little. Its very length however is eloquent enough: a child of nine came, saw, and conquered the West (or was conquered by it); it took a woman of thirty-eight—and one who already had three

7

published volumes behind her—to write *O Pioneers*, Willa Cather's first characteristic book.

From the first the conquest was final, satisfying, exultant. The following autobiographical fragment is convincing proof of this and of the coincidence between Willa Cather's discovery of the West and the awakening of her literary vocation.[1]

Willa Cather was born, 1875, near Winchester, Va., of Charles Fectigue Cather and Virginia Sibert Boak. The Cathers were Irish, the Siberts Alsatian.[2] Both families had long been settled in Virginia.

"When I was about nine Father took me from our place near Winchester, Va., to a ranch near Red Cloud, Nebraska, a little town on the Burlington Railroad named for the famous Sioux warrior. Life on a Nebraskan ranch, in those days when the country was thinly settled, was full of adventure. Farming was then a secondary matter; the most important occupation was the feeding of the great herds of cattle driven up from Texas, and most of the great prairie country from the Missouri River to Denver was still open grazing land. There was no school near at hand. I lived out of doors, winter and summer. All the near neighbors were Scandinavians, and 10 or 12 miles away there was an entire township settled by Bohemians. I had a pony and rode about the Norwegian and Bohemian settlements.[3]

"In Virginia, where the original land grants made in the reigns of George II and George III had been going down from father to son ever since, life was ordered and settled, the people in good families were born good, and the poor mountain people were not expected to amount to much. There had been no element of struggle since the Civil War. Foreigners were looked down upon, unless they were English or persons of title. An imaginative child, taken out of this definitely arranged background, and dropped down among struggling immigrants from all over the world, naturally found something to think about. Struggle appeals to a child more than comfort and picturesqueness, because it is dramatic. No child with a spark of generosity could have kept from throwing herself heart and soul into the fight these people were making to master the language, to master the soil, to hold their land and to get ahead in the world. I grew fond of some of the immigrants, particularly the old women who used to tell me of their home country. I used to think them underrated, and wanted to explain them to their neighbors. I have never found any intellectual excitement more intense than I used to feel when I spent a morning with one of these pioneer women at her baking or butter-making. *I used to ride home in the most unreasonable state of excitement.* I always felt as if they told me so much more than they said—*as if I had actually got inside another person's skin. . . .*[4] No other adventure carries one quite so far.

"Their stories used to go round and round in my head at night. *This was, with me, the initial impulse.*

"*The first two years on the ranch were probably more important to me as a writer than any that came afterward.* Every story I have written since then has been the recollection of some childhood experience, of something that touched me while a youngster. You must know a subject as a child, before you ever had any idea of writing, to instill into it, in a story, the true feeling.

"I have always had a habit of remembering mannerisms, turns of speech. The phraseology of those people stuck in my mind. If I had made notes, the material collected would be dead. No, it's memory—the memory that goes with the vocation."[5]

> *"I think that most of the basic material a writer works with is acquired before the age of fifteen.* That's the important period: when one is not writing. Those years determine whether one's work will be poor or rich. . . ."[6]

Willa Cather was soon to exchange the prairie for the schoolroom. Whatever she lost or gained in the exchange, the prairie and the pioneers had given her what no school could have given and no school could take: the first price-less experience of life in the open in a vast untamed country (an experience all the more vivid and unfor-gettable as it came to the quick sensitive young girl with all the excitement of discovery), a "love of great spaces, of rolling open countries like the sea,"[7] a habit of taking life's blessings and her blows with the pioneers' patient simplicity, a large-hearted sympathy ("as if I had actu-ally got inside another person's skin"), a wide tolerance, a strong desire—not so easily nor so soon to be satisfied —to give eloquent English tongue to the unsung beauty of the West, to the pioneers' inarticulate dreams, their stoic acceptance of the inevitable, their ready answer to the call of adventure and of the land.

Reading, meditation, toil, the maturing influence of time, the slow filling-in of the reservoirs of memory were to make this possible, and give us the masterly overtures of *O Pioneers* and *My Ántonia*. Before these could be, there were to be the first crude sentimental stories, the false start of *The Troll Garden* and *Alexander's Bridge*.

"All the while that she was racing about over the country by day, Willa Cather was reading at night. She read a good many of the English classics aloud to her two grandmothers. She learned Latin early and read it easily. Later her father moved his family into the little town of Red Cloud, and she went to the high school, but she learned her Latin from an old English gentleman, who had the enthusiasm of the true scholar, and with whom she used to read even after she entered the University of Nebraska. She was graduated from that university at nineteen . . ."[8]

Willa Cather must have come to college with Tom Outland's and Claude Wheeler's thirst for knowledge, their urgent blundering craving for an enlargement of their personalities and their experience through contact with the civilizations and the great men of the past. How much of it was satisfied? Did she find a Professor St. Peter to hasten the maturing process? Did her mind already fondly dwell on the mellow art of living, the supreme efflorescence of French culture? All this we can only surmise. The one thing we do know is that she already wrote.

"Back in the files of the College magazine, there were once several of my perfectly honest but very clumsy attempts to give the story of some of the Scandinavian and Bohemian settlers who lived not far from my father's farm . . . These early stories were bald, clumsy, and emotional."[9]

"The story of some of the Scandinavian and Bohemian settlers . . . bald, clumsy, and emotional": that Willa Cather's first stories should deal with her immigrant friends might have been expected; that they should be bald and clumsy her inexperience easily accounts for; but why should they be emotional?

They could not well have been otherwise.

Willa Cather's experience of pioneer life had been intimate and varied. She was too near it however to treat it with any measure of detachment. As she was both romantic by nature (we shall have abundant proof of it) and shy of betraying too much of herself, she was fain

to dramatize and sentimentalize,[10] with the not unnatural
result that the stories failed to satisfy her and she decided that she "wouldn't write any more about the country and the people for whom [she] had a personal
feeling."[11]

For all of eighteen years, the eighteen years that go
from her graduation (1895) to the publication of *O
Pioneers*, her first original book (1913), she persevered
in her resolution, her growing, despairing admiration for
Henry James but confirming her in it.[12]

A young writer must needs learn his craft somewhere.
As so many future novelists, from Maupassant and Zola
down to our day, have gone to school to Flaubert, or so
many new-fledged poets first tried their strength in impotent but necessary and ultimately fruitful imitation of
Spenser or of Keats, she went to Henry James to learn
how to use and to place words. She knew of course that
the delicate artificiality of his style, however perfect a
medium to convey the complex interplay of thought, perception and feeling in characters supersensitive and re-
fined, was unfit to sing the epic beauty of the West. She
had given that up. And, for all she was to say later,[13]
that she never ceased "trying to compromise between the
kind of matter that [her] experience had given [her]
and the manner of writing which [she] admired," she
never did compromise: turning a deaf ear to the sirens
that said, "Write of the West and of thyself," she chose
instead to "write well."

The result was *The Troll Garden* (1905) and *Alexander's Bridge* (1912).

But there are ten years between her graduation and
the publication of *The Troll Garden*, ten years which
Willa Cather was wise enough to spend not in writing
but in making herself worthy to write by first acquiring
an experience of people and of the world.[14] For what did
she know of the world? However deep and intense her

experience had been, it was a narrow one. Beyond pioneer
Nebraska and the college campus all was *terra incognita*
to her.

She set out in a spirit of gay adventure, going East
(and East also meant Europe), living in the East (and
in Europe), yet always coming back to the West to
breathe her own native air,[15] test East by West and
West by East, take note of the changes going on and
altering (altering for the worst, she thought) the country she knew best—for these were the fateful years when
industrial exploitation of the soil was replacing the old
open grazing, and the first generation, the pioneers and
builders with the large vision and the unbounded hopes,
were replaced by matter-of-fact small-town business
men.[16]

She wrote next to nothing, content, whether doing
journalistic work or teaching in Pittsburgh,[17] traveling
and sojourning in France, or roaming about Wyoming,
Colorado and her own Nebraska, to feel and to live,
secretly storing in memories and knowledge, taking in
those precious vignettes of French life and Spanish landscape that were to delight the reader of *One of Ours*,
The Professor's House or *Death Comes for the Archbishop*, laying by or adding to that deep intimate knowledge of the plains that was to give such strength and
substance to her books from *O Pioneers* on to her latest.

A few poems, a few stories were all the product of the
first ten of these eighteen years. She collected some of
the poems (*April Twilights*, 1903), then had the good
luck to have the manuscript of her first collection of short
stories come under the discerning eye of S. S. McClure
who published the stories (*The Troll Garden*, 1905) and,
very soon (1906) offered Willa Cather, who accepted, a
position on the staff of his magazine. Two years later
(1908) she became managing editor of *McClure's*.

Her editorial work, fortunately, proved as little ab-

sorbing as her journalistic activity and her schoolwork
had been, and Willa Cather again had time for sojourns
in Europe and in the West—the Southwest rather this
time, for it is then Willa Cather discovered Arizona and
New Mexico, listened, with what eagerness the reader of
Death Comes for the Archbishop can imagine, to tales of
the Spanish conquest and the Spanish missions and, her
heart beating like Thea Kronborg or Tom Outland's,
first came upon those sacred spots of humanity's early
history (*she* was to make us feel they were sacred), the
Indian Cliff Dwellings.

Her position on the staff of *McClure's* offered new out-
lets to her pen. She had the good sense, and the courage
—it takes courage not to write when writing comes easy
and is welcomed—still to write next to nothing. In 1911
at last, when she was thirty-six,[18] she gave up editorial
work for good and retired to work on her first novel,
which came out in 1912, first as *Alexander's Masquerade*
in *McClure's*, then in book form under its present title of
Alexander's Bridge. The book was a mediocre one. But
one year later she published *O Pioneers*, her first original
work and the first of a fast-growing series of remarkable
books.

The story of her books becomes henceforth the story
of her life. Wherever she lived now she carried all her
books in her.

III

THERE is very little of her verse and not much is of any importance. The best poems are songs of the beauty and the precariousness of life and of passion: *In Media Vita*, 1901,[1] *In Rose-Time*, 1902, or this brief impassioned outburst:

THE HAWTHORN TREE

Across the shimmering meadows—
Ah, when he came to me!
In the springtime,
In the nighttime,
In the starlight,
Beneath the hawthorn tree.

Up from the misty marshland—
Ah, when he climbed to me!
To my white bower,
To my sweet rest,
To my warm breast,
Beneath the hawthorn tree.

Ask of me what the birds sang,
High in the hawthorn tree;
What the breeze tells,
What the rose smells,
What the stars shine—
Not what he said to me!

The rest are mostly poems of conventional form and conventional symbols (minstrels, troubadours, knights, pilgrims, shepherd lads and shepherd maids, roses and pearls) or vignettes of travel, unoffending ear or taste, at best picturesque, hardly ever impressive, betraying practically nothing of their author's personality.

There is one outstanding exception in the early volume, where, as in the later *Prairie Spring* (1912) and *Macon Prairie*, Willa Cather—characteristically at her best when inspired by the West—condenses in a few blank verse lines (their briefness, directness, and consequent grandeur not unlike Chinese poetry) a whole ample landscape:

Prairie Dawn

A crimson fire that vanquishes the stars;
A pungent odor from the dusty sage;
A sudden stirring of the huddled herds;
A breaking of the distant table-lands
Through purple mists ascending, and the flare
Of water-ditches silver in the light;
A swift, bright lance hurled low across the world;
A sudden sickness for the hills of home.

Several of Willa Cather's poems strike the romantic note of the supreme beauty of passion: almost all of the short stories do.

They are not of equal merit. The feeblest—the lifeless *Marriage of Phaedra*, and those two portraits of love-lorn women, *The Garden Lodge* and *A Death in the Desert*, sentimental studies *in vacuo*—show only too clearly the net loss to Willa Cather and to her art when she renounced her sure foothold on Nebraskan earth.[2] The other stories, whether, like *A Wagner Matinée*, they show the disturbing influence of music, calling back to life and to pain a soul dulled by years of isolation and drudgery on a bleak Nebraska homestead, or, like *The Sculptor's Funeral* and *Paul's Case*,[3] center round the

contrast between an artist's or an adolescent's fervid soul
and the mean hypocritical world around him, the dead
world that would fain put out the clear flame that re-
proves its own frigidity—the other stories, however romantic, owe to the warmth of Willa Cather's vindication
of beauty and of passion and to her scathing denunciation of the world's blind complacency, moving eloquence
and a convincing reality.

More interesting, however, to my way of thinking,[4] than
any of the other *Troll Garden* stories is *Flavia and Her
Artists*, the only unromantic story in the book and a not
unworthy forerunner of *A Lost Lady*. Flavia Hamilton,
its heroine, an unbalanced, hysterical woman, aglow with
a passion for art which is but a disguise for her worldly
ambition and her absence of feeling and genuine interest
in life, finds a constantly troubled satisfaction in the
motley group of celebrities, literary and otherwise ("her
artists"), that she gathers around herself. The story,
half pathetic, half ironic, is the first of that series of
women's portraits that includes Marian Forrester, Myra
Henshawe and Rosamond St. Peter, women brilliant and
hard, childless, idle, town-bred, who stand in such strong
contrast with the Alexandras, the Antonias, the Thea
Kronborgs, the big generous natures near to the soil and
to Willa Cather's heart. Flavia's story, like those of Mrs.
Forrester, Myra Henshawe and Rosamond St. Peter, is
also a study of marriage. It is a study of the interrelation
between a selfish, more or less unbalanced wife and the
husband whose calm, unassuming presence[5] counterbal-
ances (even if it sometimes exacerbates) her hysterical
tendencies, saving her, without her suspecting it, from
many a false or a dangerous step. The greater irony of
Flavia consists in the husband sparing his wife, at the
cost of drawing her scorn and anger on himself, a revelation of "her artists' " contempt for her which alone might
have cured her.

Flavia is of interest also as being the earliest example

in Willa Cather's work of a method that was to be a favorite one with her (*My Ántonia, A Lost Lady, My Mortal Enemy*). The story is told by a youth through whose eager, sensitive eyes we see the heroine, a device which, when skilfully used,[6] greatly enhances the irony and pathos of the story.

Flavia and Her Artists, however, is better in conception than in execution. Its rather wooden style, awkward split infinitives, bookish conversations (faults shared by *The Garden Lodge* and *The Marriage of Phaedra* in the same volume and, to some extent, by *Scandal* in *Youth and the Bright Medusa*) point to the same lesson as the corresponding faults (stiffness of dialogue, lack of selection and restraint) in the other *Troll Garden* stories: Willa Cather could strive to *acquire* a style, she would only *have* one when she dared to express her deeper self. Meanwhile, the lack of vitality in some of the stories, the overstressed romanticism in the others betrayed less the writer's immaturity than the divorce between her sensibility and her art.

The tension in Willa Cather at last became intolerable. In her next work, *Alexander's Bridge*, an otherwise little remarkable book, she chose as her hero a man torn between two allegiances, as she herself was torn, a man "starving for reality"[7] as she was now starving for it.

Like *Flavia and Her Artists*, *Alexander's Bridge* was a psychological study, the portrait of a man, an engineer ("a natural force" (19), "a powerfully equipped nature" (21)), involved in a liaison with a London actress and living a double life—his calm, orderly life with his wife, a charming Boston aristocrat who satisfies her husband's taste for comfort, refinement, stability; his passionate love for the actress, not an aristocrat but a living woman.

"In his feeling for his wife there was all the tenderness,

all the pride, all the devotion of which he was capable. There was everything but energy" (144).

"He found himself living exactly the kind of life he had determined to escape. . . . Hardships and difficulties he had carried lightly: overwork had not exhausted him; but this dead calm of middle life which confronted him—of that he was afraid. He was not ready for it. It was like being buried alive. . . . The one thing he had really wanted all his life was to be free . . ." (49)

The trouble is that he dare not be free. He fails to choose between Boston and freedom, wavers on and finally ("I am not a man who can live two lives" (104)) goes to pieces as his most ambitious bridge collapses.

Alexander's Bridge is an unconvincing book. There are beautiful passages in it (London and Boston interiors, London and Boston sunsets), the book is well constructed and reads smoothly, yet Lloyd Morris's criticism of it is right. *Alexander's Bridge*, he says, is "a slight story almost flawless in form but wholly deficient in the sustaining illusion of reality."[8]

The book fails because, however real the problem that confronts its hero, he never (or hardly ever) quite comes to life, nor is his accidental death a satisfactory solution of his dilemma. The book, in other words,[9] characteristically Willa Cather's as it depicts a crisis in a man of forty ("in his dangerous middle age his unexhausted youth fermented within him"),[10] is a failure as Willa Cather does not allow her hero to "live out his potentialities" (16).

The true solution of Alexander's problem and its natural conclusion are outside the book—in Willa Cather's own life, in the momentous resolve to which we owe *O Pioneers* (published only one year after *Alexander's Bridge*) and all its followers.

The resolution was an act of courage. It meant giving up the methods and aims which had made all her former work possible.

Willa Cather was almost forty. She had been writing for twenty years. What had she to show for it? A few poems, a few stories, not so bad perhaps but certainly not good enough to satisfy either her critical judgment or the deeper exigences of her heart. Her psychological studies, *Flavia and Her Artists, Alexander's Bridge*, however honest, had an air of artificiality and their structural perfection (such as it was) was but a negative quality, proving that although Willa Cather "could do that sort of thing" as well as any other disciple of Henry James, she could not do it better than they and never as well as the master himself. Her romantic stories, though they held more promise (after all, the romantic strain was deep-rooted in her, rooted in her sensibility and in her pioneer experience), were marred by imperfections of style and by sentimental exaggeration. She had come to a dead end. Beyond *The Garden Lodge* was utter vacuity. Beyond *Flavia* and *Alexander's Bridge*, second-rate analysis of character and social life. Beyond the other stories there was hope—if only Willa Cather would at last consent to *publier sa mémoire et vous ouvrir son coeur*.[11]

She did in *O Pioneers*, and the result is sweet unto this day.

IV

IN *ALEXANDER'S BRIDGE* I was still more preoc-
cupied with trying to write well than with anything
else. It takes a great deal of experience to become natural.
People grow in honesty as they grow in anything else.
A painter or writer must learn to distinguish what is his
own from what he admires.[1] I never abandoned trying to
compromise between the kind of matter that my experience had given me and the manner of writing which I admired, until I began my second novel *O Pioneers*![2] And
from the first chapter I decided not to 'write' at all—
simply to give myself up to the pleasure of recapturing
in memory people and places I had believed forgotten.
This was what my friend Sarah Orne Jewett had advised
me to do. She said to me that if my life had lain in a part
of the world that was without a literature, and I couldn't
tell about it truthfully in the form I most admired, I
should have to make a kind of writing that would tell it,
no matter what I lost in the process."[3]

Sarah Orne Jewett was right. *O Pioneers* proves it.

Not that it is a perfect book. Structurally, it is inferior to *Alexander's Bridge* or the *Troll Garden* stories.
Partly, because, as the story was not built from the outside but "formed itself inevitably" within Willa Cather's
mind, she felt very little "power of choice about the
molding of it."[4] Partly, because in *O Pioneers* she grasped
more than she could hold.

She chose to treat a subject of epic magnitude. Taking
a pioneer woman's life as the focus of her work, she would
evoke the whole epic of pioneering days and trace to
their tragic or their happy ends the contrasted destinies
of the sons and daughters of the pioneers. Epic of the
soil, drama of passion, simple recital of human toil

crowned by tranquil happiness—the book was to be a compound of all those. No wonder if it turned out to be less powerful and less perfect as a whole than in its component parts.

It lacks indeed both unity of time and place (the tamed Nebraska of Parts II to V is quite another country from the wild Nebraska of Part I) and unity of treatment and subject. The book at first seems to be about to keep the promise of its title. Part I is a splendid overture whose dominant note is that of man's stubborn, heroic struggle against hostile nature. From the second part on, however, man having overcome at last the resistance of nature, the interest centers on the interrelations of some interesting personalities and passion comes more and more to the fore. In Parts III and IV (the most dramatic and perhaps the best) passion holds sway. Part V and last brings us back to the calm figure of the heroine (carefully kept in the background through Parts III and IV) and *l'amour-amitié* takes the place of *l'amour-passion* with consequent decrease in warmth and an unfortunate falling off of interest.

O Pioneers has still other faults. Of the two principal women characters, Alexandra, the heroine, and Marie Shabata, Alexandra, unquestionably the more original and the greater, only compels admiration when Marie wins our love. There is grandeur about Alexandra, but there is not warmth, or at least while we *know* she has fervor we do not *feel* it, and even her indomitable energy seems cold beside Marie's tragic intensity. Then there is Carl Lindstrum, an unsubstantial, unconvincing, lifeless figure . . .

An imperfect book, but a great book. Its worst defects are redeemed by its fulness of life, its epic breadth, and its truth.

"One January day, thirty years ago, the little town of Hanover, anchored on a windy Nebraska table-land, was trying not to be blown away." Such the initial notes of the symphony. In two pages, of direct presentation, not description, a bleak winter landscape has grown around us. We shuffle along the Main Street of Hanover together with country people going about their errands. A few pages more, and we know, so perfectly as to recognize them in a crowd, pretty Bohemian Marie, little Emil Bergson, his sister Alexandra, a Scandinavian beauty and a strong, decided girl, their friend Carl Lindstrum, "a thin frail boy, with brooding dark eyes, . . . a mouth too sensitive for a boy, . . . lips with already a little curl of bitterness and skepticism"—all the protagonists of the story. With them we leave the town, we are introduced to the Bergson homestead, a low log-house on a ridge, scarcely discernible from the surrounding prairie. We meet honest John Bergson and his sons ("in eleven long years John Bergson had made but little impression upon the wild land he had come to tame"), heavy, stupid Oscar, Lou, a "fussy and flighty" boy.

John Bergson dies, the boys want to give it up. Alexandra insists on holding on, and even buys more land.

This is Part I, *The Wild Land*.

Part II, *The Neighboring Fields*, opens with quite a different picture. Sixteen years have passed, fields of wheat and corn have replaced the prairie. Everybody is prosperous, Alexandra, head of the Bergson family by right of being its brains and its will power, most of all. Emil is twenty-one, an athlete, a college boy. He is in love with Marie, now the wife of irritable Frank Shabata. Oscar and Lou are married, but they are not doing so well as Alexandra and they are jealous of her. Carl Lindstrum, thirty-five now, on his way to Alaska stops at Alexandra's. "His face was intelligent, sensitive, unhappy." Country gossip makes it impossible for him to marry Alexandra. He will come back in a year's time, a rich man, and will then marry her. He goes. So does Emil who, seeing his love for Marie is hopeless, departs for Mexico.[5]

Part II has Alexandra's farm as its center of interest, but there is a whole countryside around it, with Scandinavian, Bohemian and French settlements, and a rich variety of types and customs.

Part III, *Winter Memories*, has but twenty pages, in comparison with Part I's seventy and Part II's hundred odd. It is a winter interlude of waiting—Alexandra's waiting for Carl, Marie's waiting for Emil.

Part IV, *The Mulberry Tree*, is under the sign of death. Emil has come back, more madly in love than ever, handsomer, more dangerously fascinating, for the South has given him more abandon and fire and a touch of exotic beauty. Scandinavians, Bohemians and French meet at a fête, all is love and jollity. For a brief moment Emil can clasp Marie in his arms. But death lurks behind the scenes. Harvest time and fruition of desire. Amédée, jolliest of the French boys and a hard worker, and but newly made the happiest of men, is struck down on his own harvest field; Frank Shabata, mad with jealousy, kills Emil and Marie as they lie, made one at last, under the white mulberry tree.

Part V, *Alexandra*. Alexandra has lost her assurance. Things like Emil and Marie's passion must be, she supposes, but why cannot they be helped? And what monstrous, unexpected forces are at work behind life's smooth texture, yea even within man's heart? She is bewildered, she needs an arm to lean on, a calm presence near her to restore her peace of mind. Luckily Carl comes back (he has heard the terrible news). They will marry, they will go through life hand in hand, theirs will be a sober, placid happiness.

There is a wholesome comprehensiveness about the book; the world is a beautiful world, Willa Cather seems to say. There is room in it for the snow and for the harvest, each in its season, and each good of its kind. Man's heart is a wonderful thing, whether beating with calm steady beats or throbbing with the fever of love. Emil's dissatisfaction with his surroundings is right, and so is Alexandra's intimate union with the land she has redeemed from savagery. French jolliness and swagger, Scandinavian gravity, Slavonic impulsiveness—they are all legitimate, all are enjoyable parts of the rich picture of American life . . .

Loutish Oscar, flighty Lou Bergson, Emil, restive and ardent; Frank Shabata, the prey of mean suspicions and maddening jealousy; Amédée and his friends, "spirited and jolly . . . and always delighted to hear about anything new"; crazy Ivar, a simple trusty child of nature, as defenceless and as happy as every little child cosily sheltered in the center of its own tiny universe;[6] Marie, the incarnation of passion, fire and beauty in one lovely figure made to enslave and madden men's hearts;[7] Alexandra, the strong woman of the Proverbs, resolute and energetic, with man-like intelligence, strength of body and of mind.[8] Full-length portraits or mere sketches, no weak hand drew these, no narrow mind conceived characters so diverse and so true. But one year before they were born the same hand was writing *Alexander's Bridge*!

"And from the first chapter I decided not to 'write' at all." Willa Cather's wise decision gave *O Pioneers* not only the life and truth that *Alexander's Bridge* so completely lacked, it made it possible for the writing to become "so lost in the object that it doesn't exist for the reader—except for the reader who knows how difficult it is to lose writing in the object."[9] Style, in other words, was no longer, as in the earlier stories, a thing to be sought out for itself. It came, inevitably and unobtrusively, as the result of clear vision and genuine emotion truthfully rendered. It is not always perfect (Willa Cather's ear and taste[10] are sometimes at fault), yet, as the passage below will prove, it has, on the whole, astonishing limpidity.

"They had made an early start one morning and had driven a long way before noon. When Emil said he was hungry, they drew back from the road, gave Brigham his oats among the bushes, and climbed up to the top of a grassy bluff to eat their lunch under the shade of some little elm trees. The river was clear there, and shallow, since there had been no rain, and it ran in ripples over the sparkling sand. Under the overhanging willows of the opposite bank there was an inlet where the water was deeper and flowed so slowly that it seemed to sleep in the sun. In this little bay a single wild duck was swimming and diving and preening her feathers, disporting herself very happily in the flickering light and shade. They sat for a long time watching the solitary bird take its pleasure. No living thing had ever seemed to Alexandra as beautiful as that wild duck. Emil must have felt about it as she did, for afterward, when they were at home, he used sometimes to say, 'Sister, you know our duck down there ——' Alexandra remembered that day as one of the happiest in her life. Years afterward she thought of the duck as still there, swimming and diving all by herself in the sunlight, a kind of enchanted bird that did not know age or change."[11]

"Meditative pathos." "Emotion recollected in tranquillity." The Wordsworth touch is also Willa Cather's, and this is, if I am not mistaken, its first appearance in her work.

Thus, however imperfect (its imperfections such as would kill a smaller book), *O Pioneers* lives as a work of truth and of restrained emotion.

V

SO ALSO does *The Song of the Lark* (1915), Willa
Cather's next book, a work also marked by defects
in structure, but having over *O Pioneers* the advantage
of having but one central figure and one who unites Marie
Shabata's beauty and fire with Alexandra's determined
strength.

A longer and a fuller book than *O Pioneers, The Song
of the Lark* takes us through nearly five hundred crowded
pages from Thea Kronborg's early youth in Moonstone,
Colorado, to her twenty-seventh year or so, the year of
her first triumphs as a Wagner singer at the Metropolitan Opera.

Willa Cather has a tender spot for musicians.[1] Of all
musicians, however, operatic singers seem to interest her
the most. She must have met many in Pittsburgh and in
New York, big personalities all, it seems, without calcu-
lation or meanness, eccentric perhaps, but with astonishing generosity of feeling and extraordinary gusto. There
are portraits or sketches of them in several of her works.
The German Wagner singer in *One of Ours*, Kitty Ayrshire and Cressida Garnett in *Youth and the Bright
Medusa*.[2]

The Song of the Lark, the story of such a singer, is
an "account of how a Moonstone girl found her way out
of a vague, easy-going world into a life of disciplined
endeavor" (480). It begins with Thea Kronborg, a little
girl lying ill in bed and, but for the accidental intervention of her friend Dr. Archie, very nearly dying of pneu-
monia. Her mother has been delivered of a child, her
seventh, and her father, the Rev. Peter Kronborg, forgets
all about Thea's "cold" in his excitement over the new
baby. How precarious a thing is genius, how marvelous

that it ever lives at all![3] Thea's father is a Swedish
Methodist minister, a farmer's son who has drifted into
the ministry for no visible reason except laziness, an in-
capacity to do a man's work and an unconscious aptitude
for getting on well with women. An honest man withal,
dull, pompous, sincere, a good husband and a good
father.[4] No personality. Not so Mrs. Kronborg, an intensely practical woman, calm, firm, with a head on her
shoulders, a respect for facts, a way of managing her
family and her husband with a minimum of interference
and of fuss.

> "Although she was so enmeshed in family cares
> most of the time, she could emerge serene when she
> was away from them. For a mother of seven, she had
> a singularly unprejudiced point of view. She was,
> moreover, a fatalist, and as she did not attempt to
> direct things beyond her control, she found a good
> deal of time to enjoy the ways of man and nature"
> (99).

She certainly enjoys Thea's unfolding, sees that she
has what quiet and seclusion are to be had in a crowded
house. "She found her more interesting than her other
children, and she took her more seriously, without thinking much about why she did so" (65). Thea has her
mother's splendid physique, her commonsense, her untir-
ing energy, her complete absence of littleness and of sham.
Her ear for music she also owes to Mrs. Kronborg.

At first Thea is only a happy, passionate little girl,
roaming the hills in search of bright stones. She has, however, that rare combination of gifts, an imagination and
a will. Her imagination (and sensitiveness) she shows
very early, best of all perhaps when, being one day in
Wyoming with her father, an old ranchman takes them
to "a ridge up in the hills called Laramie Plain, where

the wagon-trails of the Forty-niners and the Mormons were still visible:

> "All the way there was much talk of the Forty-niners . . . of Indians and buffalo, thirst and slaughter, wanderings in snowstorms, and lonely graves in the desert . . .
>
> "The top of the ridge, when they reached it, was a great flat plain, strewn with white boulders, with the wind howling over it. There was not one trail, as Thea had expected; there were a score; deep furrows, cut in the earth by heavy wagon wheels, and now grown over with dry, whitish grass . . . They were, indeed, only old wagon ruts, running east and west, and grown over with grass. But as Thea ran about among the white stones, her skirts blowing this way and that, the wind brought to her eyes tears that might have come anyway . . . To the west one could see range after range of blue mountains, and at last the snowy range, with its white, windy peaks, the clouds caught here and there on their spurs . . . The wind never slept on this plain, the old man said. Every little while eagles flew over" (54).

"She hated difficult things, and yet she could never pass one by" (96): Thea's obstinacy, as characteristic of her as her sensitiveness, is first seen at its best in the way she works at her music:

> "Professor Wunsch went to the houses of his other pupils to give them their lessons, but one morning he told Mrs. Kronborg that Thea had talent, and that if she came to him he could teach her in his slippers, and that would be better. Mrs. Kronborg was a strange woman. That word 'talent,' which no one else in Moonstone, not even Dr. Archie, would have un-

derstood, she comprehended perfectly. To any other woman there, it would have meant that a child must have her hair curled every day and must play in public. Mrs. Kronborg knew it meant that Thea must practice four hours a day" (24-25).

Old Wunsch, one of Willa Cather's best creations, is a German musician. A wreck of a musician and of a man. He has drifted into Moonstone from nowhere and will drift away again. He is a drunkard, a pedant, but he was once a living man, and he shows occasional signs of his former ambition and his youthful fire. He is the first to find out Thea's talent, that mixture of stubbornness and imagination, that strange passion which makes the difference between her and the innumerable little American misses he has had to teach. Wunsch teaches her "according to the old Stuttgart method; stiff back, stiff elbows, a very formal position of the hands." No matter; with Wunsch she develops "an unusual power of work" (174-5).

Deep concealed in Thea's heart is a desire to be a singer. Wunsch, by some intuition incomprehensible to Thea, divines her secret. Himself still capable of emotion when he thinks of a great operatic singer he heard in his youth (the passage, pp. 72-73 of the book, has singular pathos, a beauty achieved by transfiguration of the almost grotesque into emotion), Wunsch quickens the little flame burning in Thea's heart. Having, by some impatient, half-scornful questions, tried the solidity of Thea's vocation, the subtlety of her intuition, the ardor of the passion in her,[5] he comes out one day with the memorable words, a trumpet call to Thea, "Nothing is far and nothing is near, if one desires. . . . There is only one big thing—desire. And before it, when it is big, all is little . . ." (76).

These are about the last sensible words Wunsch has to

say. He soon gets dead drunk, raves about like a mad-
man (a powerful scene) and finally leaves the town, leav-
ing his pupils to Thea, now a girl of thirteen, strangely
mature for her age and the best musician in Moonstone.

Wunsch gone, Thea has still three friends left, her
mother, Dr. Archie, Ray Kennedy.

Dr. Archie, the Moonstone doctor, is a young man of
about thirty when Thea is eleven. Tied by an early marriage to a wife who is the incarnation of meanness and
avarice ("he had married Belle White because he was
romantic—too romantic to know anything about women,
except what he wished them to be" (86)[6]), too shy and
too proud to divorce her, Dr. Archie finds a refuge in
his vocation, in his books, in occasional potations, in
flights to Denver and easy women, and, above all, though
he hardly knows why he is so fond of the little girl, in his
friendship for Thea. He will help her later, in critical
moments of her life. At Moonstone he lends her books,
discusses life with her, enjoys her spontaneity, her energy,
the passion she puts into everything she does. Like
Wunsch, whom Thea's uncompromising ardor made at
times ashamed of the hopeless mess he had made of his
life, Dr. Archie is both thrilled and humiliated by Thea's
zest. For the first time he realizes that a man has only
"about twenty able, waking years" and that "the main
thing is to live those twenty splendid years" (138-9).
Thea realizes it also. After her long earnest talks with
him, she feels "happy, flattered and stimulated . . . She
had only twenty years—no time to lose" (139-40).

No time to lose. Not Dr. Archie, but death suddenly
makes her fully aware of it. Two brutal deaths, a tramp's,
Ray Kennedy's.

"Early in July, soon after Thea's fifteenth birthday,
a particularly disgusting sort of tramp came into Moonstone in an empty box car" (135). Moonstone holds its
nose and ejects the pitiful starving wretch. "A week after

the tramp excitement had passed over, the city water
began to smell and to taste." A fever breaks out, "several
adults and half a dozen children" die of it. "The tramp
had got even with Moonstone. He had climbed the stand-
pipe by the handholds and let himself down into seventy-
five feet of cold water . . ." (135-7). The gruesome
episode is the first, grotesque intrusion of tragedy in
Thea's happy world. Ray Kennedy's death is the next.

"There was a worthy man in Moonstone who was
already planning to marry Thea as soon as she
should be old enough. His name was Ray Kennedy,
his age was thirty, and he was conductor on a freight
train, his run being from Moonstone to Denver. Ray
was a big fellow, with a square, open American face,
a rock chin, and features that one would never happen to remember. He was an aggressive idealist, a
freethinker, and, like most railroad men, deeply
sentimental" (46).

Ray takes Thea and her family on drives to the sand-
hills, or on trips to Denver in his calaboose, tells Thea
stories of his life as shepherd or railroad man, tales of
mining adventures, tales of good luck and bad in the
Southwest and in old Mexico, tales of the Indian Cliff
Dweller remains he has come to know in the course of his
vagrant existence. But never does he speak of his hopes.

"He had the chivalry which is perhaps the proud-
est possession of his race. He had never embarrassed
her by so much as a glance. . . . He . . . never
touched her. . . . His blue eyes were clear and shallow, friendly, uninquiring. He rested Thea because
he was so different; because, though he often told her
interesting things, he never set lively fancies going in
her head; because he never misunderstood her, and

because he never, by any chance, for a single instant, understood her! Yes, with Ray she was safe; by him she would never be discovered!" (109).

Ray is severely wounded in a railway accident. He dies, holding Thea's hand. "He would have liked to tell her a little about his old dream . . . but to tell her now would somehow be unfair; wouldn't be quite the straightest thing in the world" (148).

The world is a hard world. Life is given to men under conditions that make it necessary for one to justify one's right to live by being every inch alive, by living for the best that is in one. Thus Thea, clenching her teeth. She is ready to face the world now, to prove herself what she is. Ray's death gives her a chance. It suddenly comes out that his life was insured for six hundred dollars in Thea's favor, the money to be used to give Thea a winter of study in Chicago. After much discussion the Kronborgs agree to let Thea go. Dr. Archie will accompany her, find rooms for her, get her a good teacher. This is the end of her childhood. She must go forth, cast off Moonstone. "She had left very little. Everything that was essential seemed to be right there with her" (157).

In Chicago Thea finds it very hard at first. Dr. Archie has done his best for her, found her decent lodgings, a part-time job as singer in a Swedish church, the best piano teacher in Chicago. She is not happy. She is poor, clumsy, an ignorant country girl now first aware of the incredible extent of her ignorance.

"Every artist," Harsanyi, her music teacher, says to her one day,

"every artist makes himself born. It is very much harder than the other time, and longer. Your mother did not bring anything into the world to play piano.

That you must bring into the world yourself"
(175-6).

She works desperately, madly. She has her moments of
exultation, but is mostly unsatisfied, wretchedly miserable.
"She had come to Chicago to be with it [her vocation],
and it had deserted her" (177).

One day, by mere chance, Harsanyi discovers that she
has a voice—and what a voice!

> "He put his hand back to her throat and sat with
> his head bent, his one eye closed. He loved to hear a
> big voice throb in a relaxed, natural throat, and he
> was thinking that no one had ever felt this voice
> vibrate before . . . No one knew that it had come,
> or even that it existed; least of all the strange crude
> girl in whose throat it beat its passionate wings . . .
> ". . . She sang from the bottom of herself . . . A
> relaxed throat, a voice that lay on the breath, that
> had never been forced off the breath; it rose and fell
> in the air-column like the little balls which are put to
> shine in the jet of a fountain" (187-8).

Thea can never find herself by playing the piano; she
can only find herself, *give* herself, as a singer.

> " 'Let us talk frankly now. We have never done
> so before, and I have respected your reticence. What
> you want more than anything in the world is to be an
> artist; is that true?'
> "She turned her face away from him and looked
> down at the keyboard.
> "Her answer came in a thickened voice. 'Yes, I
> suppose so.'
> " 'When did you first feel that you wanted to be
> an artist?'
> " 'I don't know. There was always—something.'

" 'Did you never think that you were going to sing?'

" 'Yes.'

" 'How long ago was that?'

" 'Always, until I came to you. It was you who made me want to play piano.' Her voice trembled. 'Before, I tried to think I did, but I was pretending' " (209).

Harsanyi reluctantly gives Thea over to the best voice specialist in Chicago, Bowers, a cold mean nature, but the technician Thea needs to train her voice.

After a brief, unsatisfactory vacation in Moonstone—Thea's brothers and sisters have grown into coarse ordinary youths, they are jealous of her, shocked by her associating with disreputable Mexicans—Thea goes to work under Bowers. It is her hardest time. Harsanyi has gone to New York, she has only Bowers, who teaches her much but taints with his pettiness and scorn everything round Thea. She grows cynical. She becomes a pessimist. For the first time she finds herself the target of base desires, first resents the vulgarity, showiness, materialism of Bowers' semi-professional pupils ("they were usually ladies with very rich husbands, and Bowers called them the 'pampered jades of Asia' " (251). Chicago becomes to discontented Thea "the rich, noisy city, fat with food and drink" (265).

Enter Fred Ottenburg, that unusual combination (possibly to be met in real life, not easily convincing in art) the beer prince—he becomes head of the Brewers' Trust by and by—the dandy, the lady-killer, the dilettante, and the *cavaliere servento* of artists. A pupil and a friend of Bowers', he meets Thea, becomes interested in her, begins to play *deus ex machina* to the story and to her. He takes Thea in hand, gives her useful hints as to manners and dresses, gets people of his own class to take an interest in her, takes her out to suppers, and, noticing how tired she looks after her hard winter in Chicago, finally sends her off to a ranch he has in Arizona, a ranch with "a whole canyon full of Cliff-Dweller ruins" (289).

"So far she had failed. Her two years in Chicago had not resulted in anything. She had failed with Harsanyi, and she had made no great progress with her voice. She had come to believe that whatever Bowers had taught her was of secondary importance, and that in the essential things she had made no advance . . . Failure was not so tragic as she would have supposed; she was tired enough not to care" (296).

And so Thea accepts Fred Ottenburg's providential (all too providential) offer and goes to Panther Canyon, Arizona, for three summer months.

What a change from the turmoil and struggle of the big city! Up in the "deep groove running along the sides of the canyon . . . the Ancient People had built their houses . . ., a nest in a high cliff, full of sun" (297-8). Stretched out on the warm rock, looking on to "the blue air-river between the canyon walls" (301), idly following the swallows' arrow flight, Thea becomes "a mere receptacle for heat." She is released from earthly cares. She has recaptured her childhood. Nature plays on her again. Nature, but a nature humanized by the toil, the pleasures, the sufferings of the Ancient People whose invisible presence Thea feels round her. She goes back not to her own past alone, but to the past of the race. Climbing up the water trail to the cliff city, wandering among the empty houses, picking up potsherds with "graceful geometrical patterns" (305), she begins to waken from her trance.

"It seemed to Thea . . . that certain feelings were transmitted to her, suggestions that were simple, insistent, and monotonous, like the beating of Indian drums. They were not expressible in words, but seemed rather to translate themselves into atti-

tudes of body, into degrees of muscular tension or
relaxation; the naked strength of youth, sharp as the
sunshafts; the crouching timorousness of age, the
sullenness of women who waited for their captors.
At the first turning of the canyon there was a half-
ruined tower of yellow masonry, a watch-tower upon
which the young men used to entice eagles and snare
them with nets. Sometimes for a whole morning Thea
could see the coppery breast and shoulders of an
Indian youth there against the sky; see him throw
the net, and watch the struggle with the eagle"
(302-3).

She comes to understand what water meant to those
people, the why and wherefore of the pottery, "their most
direct appeal to water, the envelope and sheath of the
precious element itself . . . The stream and the broken
pottery: what was any art but an effort to make a sheath,
a mold in which to imprison for a moment the shining,
elusive element which is life itself—life hurrying past us
and running away, too strong to stop, too sweet to lose?
. . . In singing, one made a vessel of one's throat and
nostrils and held it on one's breath, caught the stream
in a scale of natural intervals" (303-4).

There are no finer pages in Willa Cather. Deep, subtle,
of a grave, penetrating beauty, born of the Conradian
(or Pascalian) perception of the solidarity of all men in
frailty and in the mysterious power in us (call it intelligence, will power, art, or soul . . .) that transcends mor-
tality. "They had not only expressed their desire, but
they had expressed it as beautifully as they could. Food,
fire, water, and something else—even here, in this crack
in the world, so far back in the night of the past! Down
here at the beginning that painful thing was already
stirring; the seed of sorrow, and of so much delight"
(305).

Thea can go back now. She has that within her heart

that the world cannot take from her. She feels herself
carried upon a mighty stream of desire whose sources go
back to the first stirring of conscious life on this earth.
She may still fail, she knows at least what she is fighting
for.

The trouble is that she does not go back, not for quite
a while, and that, instead of launching her into life, Willa
Cather launches her into romance and melodrama. The
intensity and beauty of the canyon episode had made us
forget its artificiality: its unforeseen *dénouement* brutally
brings it home to us.

Before she accepted Fred Ottenburg's offer to send her
to Panther Canyon for two or three months Thea said to
him: ". . . It's *too* easy. Doesn't sound probable. I'm
not used to getting things for nothing" (290). She voices
our objection. It *is* too easy. It does *not* sound probable.
Rich young men like Fred Ottenburg don't give providential vacations to young girls for nothing. Answered
Fred Ottenburg: "You won't get this for nothing, quite.
I'll ask you to let me stop off and see you on my way to
California."

Two months pass without Fred Ottenburg coming—the
two months necessary for Willa Cather to bring Thea
from jadedness to renewed strength, from depression to
buoyancy, from a losing battle against the world to relaxation, command of herself, deeper understanding of
life and of art. When Fred Ottenburg at last comes Thea
is another, stronger Thea, ready for action, armed for
victory. She has made up her mind. She is not going back
to Chicago. She is "going to Germany to study without
further loss of time" (307).

Fred comes and is welcomed. Another month elapses,
a month of play in and about the canyon. The curtain
drops as Fred and Thea go down to Mexico City to be
married.

What has happened? Thea is not even madly in love with Fred Ottenburg. As he himself says to her once: "Do you know, I've decided that you never do a single thing without an ulterior motive . . . You ride and fence and walk and climb, but I know that all the while you're getting somewhere in your mind. All these things are instruments; and I, too, am an instrument" (315). Which is strictly true. Thea Kronborg then agrees to marry Fred Ottenburg out of gratitude, affection, and, well—interest. Rather a come-down after the heights of the canyon episode, but at least an unsentimental act, not out of keeping with Thea's character.

But why should Fred want to marry Thea? He is not passionately in love with her. He could wait two months before he came to share her solitude; when he does come he behaves more like an elder brother than like a lover. Not only does he know that he is but an instrument in Thea's hands, he chuckles over the fact, as if it were a particularly good joke. As a matter of fact he is as difficult to believe in as a lover as he is as a man. He is not a man. As undersexed as most of the heroes of contemporary novels are oversexed (and yet Willa Cather would have us imagine him a professional lady-killer!), to be credible he should be seventy . . .

But what if there should be a sufficient reason behind Fred's extraordinary self-restraint? There is, though we only hear of it—a cheap coup de théâtre if ever there was one!—as Fred and Thea are speeding Mexico-wards to be married. Fred Ottenburg is already married, tied to a hysterical wife whom he cannot divorce and with whom he cannot live. Thanks to this ingenious device, Fred's restraint in the first months of his acquaintance with Thea becomes the chivalrous generosity of a man who knows himself not to be free, his final proposal of marriage to her the triumph of ill-advised but sincere passion over heroic scruples. Fred, however, cannot bear to deceive Thea. Some time on the return journey from Mexico (whether he has married Thea, Willa Cather discreetly leaves in the dark) Fred confesses to Thea. Thea forgives him but leaves him. She will go to Germany on Dr. Archie's money . . . Which is all as it should be, very neat, and very artificial.

How could Willa Cather stoop to use such tricks? Not only is the whole absurd story out of keeping with the beautiful canyon episode which it is tacked on to, it very nearly ruins it, casting as it does a doubt on the sincerity and depth of Thea's but newly-strengthened convictions and certitudes, making them appear the shallow enthusiasm of an hour. Why didn't Willa Cather see that? Not an easy question to answer since we have but surmises and guesses to go by. Yet it is a question that must needs be answered—that *can* be answered, conjecturally at least, if we think of the fact that *The Song of the Lark* is only Willa Cather's second full-length novel and that it must have presented many difficulties and problems for her which only a more experienced novelist could have solved.

The novelist's craft calls for gifts not always found together. Besides the essential gift, that of creating life, your novelist must have others. He must be able to tell a good story, to paint good portraits and landscapes, his characters and his intrigue must be such as will bear critical inspection, pass successfully the test of credibility and of truth. In Willa Cather, who has the essential gift (didn't she create such well-defined personalities as Alexandra Bergson or Thea Kronborg?), the analyst and technician were at first much inferior to the narrator and to the landscape and portrait painter. She could manage the short story (the *Troll Garden* stories and *Alexander's Bridge* are structurally perfect) but the more unwieldy novel still resisted her. We saw that in *O Pioneers*, noticed the break between the first part and the rest of the book, deplored the anti-climax effect of the last chapters. In *My Ántonia*, Willa Cather's third original novel, we shall find the same defects of structure.

Willa Cather's "earlier novels seem not to have grown from a germ but to have been put together,"[7] *awkwardly* put together. Prof. Whipple's remark is true of *The Song of the Lark* as well as of its successor and its predecessor.

One can well imagine *The Song of the Lark* as having come to Willa Cather as a series of visions: Thea at Moonstone, Thea struggling in Chicago, Thea in Panther Canyon, going back to her youth and to her deeper self, Thea singing at the Metropolitan Opera, visions of inescapable clarity and truth, absolutely convincing.

Willa Cather's trouble began when she had to piece the visions together. That called for other gifts, the logician's, the analyst's. Being neither, Willa Cather went to work painfully, deserted by her inspiration, misled by sentimentality once more. To give Panther Canyon to Thea she invented Fred Ottenburg. To reward Fred Ottenburg's generosity she gave him Thea's love. But, as the vision clearly showed Thea, once the canyon episode was over, once more treading the narrow, rising path of art, Fred Ottenburg had to go, and Willa Cather concocted the absurd story we know.

Willa Cather's is no unusual case. It is always difficult for a young writer, even if he has overcome the temptation of sentimentality, to paint a character foreign to his experience. His first successful work is apt to be self-portraiture, or at least books in which the really living figures will be more or less direct duplicates of himself. When the writer is a woman, and especially a woman with strong romantic tendencies as we have seen Willa Cather to be, she will find it particularly difficult to achieve masculine characters. Intuition, self-observation, experience will help her to paint convincing women—either

protagonists or secondary figures—more or less idealized or simplified counterparts of herself (Alexandra,
Thea, Ántonia, Willa Cather's first heroines, are all cases
to the point), or, secondary figures all, foils to the
heroine, embodiments of the faults and vices she hates
(Anna Kronborg, Mrs. Archie, etc.). When it comes to
painting a man, and especially to making him the hero
worthy to stand by the heroine, the woman writer's almost irresistible tendency[8] will be to paint an ideal figure,
to achieve either a "ladies' hero" (Fred Ottenburg, George
Sand's heroes) or, if the writer is aware of her tendencies
and is on her guard, or if she have a taste for the sinister
and the melodramatic, a villain or pseudo-villain (Mr.
Rochester in *Jane Eyre*). Astonishing creatures both of
them, with little foundation in reality, and a characteristic insufficiency, or as characteristic exaggeration, of
the so-called manly virtues, the physical strength,
tenacity of purpose, energy, sensuality, etc., supposed to
be the apanage of men. A woman artist's progress might
thus be measured by her ability to paint characters more
and more foreign to her own experience, and, the crown-
ing achievement, a portrait of a man whom men will
recognize as such.

The theory will stand verification in Willa Cather's
case, accounting as it does both for her first living protagonists being all women (and women with an experience not unlike her own), and for the woodenness and
insignificance of the corresponding masculine figures:
Alexander, Carl Lindstrum, and, above all, Fred Ottenburg. Her progress too will be interesting to follow, from
O Pioneers, The Song of the Lark, My Ántonia, where the
dominant figure is in every case a woman; through *One
of Ours*, with its full-length portrait of a young man;
The Professor's House, which besides having remarkable
portraits of women (and women utterly different from
either Willa Cather's first heroines or Willa Cather herself) has the full round portrait of a man; to *Death Comes*

for the Archbishop with its two masterly male characters, Father Latour and Father Joseph.

With the canyon episode *The Song of the Lark* is practically over. There are still one hundred and fifty pages to come, it is true; Thea's departure for Germany on Dr. Archie's money, and her return to New York, seven years later, to sing at the Metropolitan Opera. Through conversations between Dr. Archie and Fred (they have become fast friends now that Dr. Archie has lost his wife, and left Moonstone and the practice of his art for Denver and business) we learn something of Thea's struggle in Germany, her mother's death and her plans and ambitions. At last we see Thea herself, in her hotel apartment and on the stage, and finally witness her triumph as an interpreter of *Fricka* and *Sieglinde*.

There are still some beautiful scenes (the scene, for example, when Thea, having come home tired and cross, is suddenly called upon to "come down and finish *Sieglinde*" (436), the famous singer who is singing the part having broken down at the end of the first act), but *The Song of the Lark* never recovers from the falsity of the *dénouement* of the canyon episode. Willa Cather seems to have lost her sure hold of her subject and of our attention. We see less and less of Thea herself, more and more of Thea as seen by Dr. Archie and Fred Ottenburg. Her struggling days are over. We do not accompany her to Germany, and, when she comes back, her fight for recognition by the leaders of the Metropolitan Opera is as nothing in comparison with her fight against herself and against the world in her Chicago days. Then like *O Pioneers* and *My Ántonia, The Song of the Lark desinit in piscem.* Not only is the last part less interesting than the rest but the book does not even end on the powerful and beautiful scene of Thea's first great triumph ("She felt like a tree bursting into bloom. And her voice was as flexible as her body; equal to any demand, capable of every *nuance*").[9] A superfluous episode brings us back to Moonstone and to the grotesque figure of Thea's Aunt Tillie.

Yet of *The Song of the Lark* as of *O Pioneers*, and with more reason still, we can say that it is a great book. A great book, and a very rich one. A masterly study, in its first three hundred pages at least, of the artistic temperament and of its building, an unforgettable evocation of the desert (page after page of the first part flashes with the hard dry colors of the Colorado desert), of the small town "set out in the sand and lightly shaded by gray-green tamarisks and cottonwoods . . . , the light-reflecting, wind-loving trees of the desert, whose roots are always seeking water and whose leaves are always talking about it, making the sound of rain" (37), of the sheer drop of the canyon, its "great wash of air" (320), its human memories.

There is youth in the book, its delight in itself, its adventures, its bitterness and its doubt. There is a warm sympathy for the "foreigners in our midst," the Germans, Mexicans, Hungarians, with their sensitiveness to music, the natural harmony of "their movements, their greetings, their low conversation, their smiles" (230); a corresponding criticism of American life with its fear of expression, its habits of hasty classification, its contempt for the simplicity and spontaneity of the Mexicans: a criticism all the more striking as it is couched in very moderate terms. There is a great, ennobling feeling of solidarity with the past, a feeling typically Willa Cather's, born of the deep, complex emotion that rises in her when she contemplates the vast Western landscape, a landscape great and awesome in itself, but made greater and more impressive to her by memory, and intense visualization, of man's passage upon it.[10]

Then there is that gallery of living individualities grouped around the central figure—Mr. and Mrs. Kronborg and Thea's brothers and sister, Aunt Tillie, Dr.

Archie, Old Wunsch, his friends the Kohlers, living a peaceful, harmonious life in the shade of the European lindens they have made to bloom in the desert, Ray Kennedy, the Tellemantez, the Chicago Swedish pastor (he might have come straight out of *Elmer Gantry*!), Harsanyi, Bowers, Fred's Jewish friends the Nathanmeyers, people of taste and of means with an intelligent and passionate interest in the arts . . . Their milieus have the same air of reality. Characters and environment are in harmony, both stand out in striking outline, the characters, seldom analyzed, unfolding themselves in dialogue and in action.

The greatest of them, the most *nuancé*, is of course Thea herself. Though not a complex figure (Willa Cather hardly drew one until she created Prof. St. Peter), Thea has the fulness and variety of life. Like most of Willa Cather's heroes and heroines[11] she has both beauty and strength, the beauty and strength of a healthy, full-blooded animal. No weak intellectual she. In fact she is not an intellectual at all. The world around her, the meaning of nature and of life she never grasps with her intelligence. She divines and feels. Neither very quick nor very bright, when in trouble she painfully works her way out. By sheer Scandinavian doggedness[12] and an unperturbed concentration on the goal she has set before herself she carries her points. She never turns an obstacle, she charges at it. She makes up her mind to become an operatic singer. Neither family ties nor love must stand in her way.[13] Once she has set her heart on something she is like a mastiff or bulldog whose jaws you cannot force open. Egotism carried so far compels admiration, it is not usually provocative of any tender emotions. Yet, as witness Ray Kennedy's, Dr. Archie's, Harsanyi's or Fred Ottenburg's experience in the book, men not only admire Thea (their weaker natures bowing to her strength), they actually love her. For Thea *is* lovable. She is lovable because she is so intensely alive, so constantly "pulsing with ardor and anticipation" (140); lovable also because, however ruthless her devotion to her aims, her ideal is a high one, and there is no littleness in her, only an unqualified giving of herself to the realization of the best in her; lovable because of her quick instinctive appreciation of passion and of beauty, her utter disregard of prejudice and conventions,[14] her powerful and delicate imagination . . .

VI

HAVING dwelt so long on *The Song of the Lark*—not only an important work but a typical example of both the shortcomings and the beauties of Willa Cather's earlier novels—I may, not unfairly, give less space to *My Ántonia*, its less ambitious successor.

The book has been extravagantly praised, H. L. Mencken calling it the best novel by an American woman. Latrobe Carroll (writing, it is true, in 1921, when neither *One of Ours*, *The Professor's House*, nor *Death Comes for the Archbishop* were in existence) proclaimed it Willa Cather's most powerful work. The truth is that *My Ántonia*, though a lifelike portrait of a pioneer girl and, in its first part at least, a striking collection of vignettes,[1] is inferior to *O Pioneers* in warmth of passion, to *The Song of the Lark* in variety and scope of interest, and has the defects in structure of both.

Like them it begins well, one hundred and fifty pages evoking in strong, direct prose the difficulties and joys of pioneer days, more particularly as exemplified in the fortunes of the Shimerdas, a family of Bohemian settlers newly arrived in Nebraska. The elder generation (melancholy Mr. Shimerda, sour grumbling Mrs. Shimerda) never get used to the incredibly primitive conditions in the new country. Their children, on the contrary, that is, first and foremost, Ántonia, take to the new land with the greater adaptability of their age, and fall to the tremendous task of making it habitable and fruitful with almost superhuman doggedness. In these pages (Book I, *The Shimerdas* of *My Ántonia*) Willa Cather reaches (though she does not surpass) the high level of the first part of *O Pioneers*. With Ántonia we roam the boundless

47

prairie, lost in the tall "shaggy red grass . . . , the color of wine stains" (16); we drift along the "dewy, heavy-odored cornfields" (156); perched "on the slanting roof of the chicken-house" we watch, on summer nights, the lightning break "in great zigzags across the heavens," or "hear the felty beat of the raindrops on the soft dust of the farmyard" (158-9). We visit Ántonia in the Shimerdas' hovel of a sod-house, Mr. Shimerda's dignified presence giving us a glimpse of an older, mellower, soberer world, the mysterious, almost mythical world over the seas. With Ántonia we call at Russian Peter and Pavel's, in open-mouth wonder watch Russian Peter eating melons uncountable, the juice trickling from his greedy mouth "down on to his curly beard" (39). On winter nights, while drifts accumulate outside and the world is a blur of spilling snow, snugly sitting round the old stove in the Burdens' basement kitchen, with Ántonia we listen to wonderful stories—stories of "gray wolves and bears in the Rockies, wildcats and panthers in the Virginia mountains" (77), and, best of all, the terrible, fascinating story of the bride thrown over to the wolves by Russian Peter and Pavel.

The pages have the freshness, vitality and beauty of the country and the days they recreate. Yet it is chiefly through Ántonia that they live, Ántonia, an eager, passionate bit of womankind, strong as an ox and as stubborn, tenacious and ambitious, generous and impulsive, a tall sturdy girl, a future mother of generations.

A peasant Thea, her deep-rooted virtues can only blossom out in the country, on the big flat wind-swept table-land where there is space around her, room for her to play unconstrained and free and write upon the horizon the great simple gestures of man wringing his bread from the earth. In the town, where Parts II and III of the book soon take her, Ántonia is under a cloud, we lose sight of her in the crowd of chattering servant girls of which she is now part. For some two hundred pages (Book II, *The Hired Girls*, Book III, *Lena Lingard*, Book IV, *The Pioneer Woman's Story*) we see but little of her, until, towards the end of the book, we meet her once more, the mother of almost a dozen children, "a battered woman now" (398), but intensely alive as ever.

A strong personality is Ántonia, a strong personality yet, like Thea Kronborg, a very simple one, and so, for all her strength—strength of physique, strength of character, strongly-defined idiosyncrasies—only in her own natural habitat can she hold our attention and capture our emotion. Willa Cather knew it. No sooner does she take Ántonia to the town, a small town in the prairie, than she tries to focus the reader's attention on Ántonia's friends, the other hired girls. The attempt is a vain one. We cannot forget Ántonia, and the book has become out of focus for the sake of two hundred dull pages concerning secondary characters whom we care little about. How could Willa Cather fail to see that with Ántonia's personality and Ántonia's conquest of the soil, her whole book stood and fell?

Her old enemy, sentimentality, her new friend, realism, here combined to blind her.

Sentimentality, Willa Cather had subdued without crushing it quite. But little apparent in *O Pioneers*,[2] in *The Song of the Lark* with Fred Ottenburg it raised its triumphant head again. But how did it creep into *My Ántonia?* Ántonia stood firm and sturdy, of the earth earthy, proof against the monster's touch. There was no weak spot in her. There was one in her creator. When Willa Cather, having written her first one hundred pages, looked upon her work and found it good, the tempter rose at her shoulder and whispered: "A brave, hardy creature this, but what about feminine charm?" Willa Cather resumed her work, and this is the picture she painted— Ántonia doing a man's work, breaking sod with the oxen, growing coarser every day:

"Her outgrown cotton dress switched about her calves, over the boot-tops. She kept her sleeves rolled up all day, and her arms and throat were burned as brown as a sailor's. Her neck came up strongly out of her shoulders, like the bole of a tree out of the turf" (140).

High time Ántonia remembered she is but fifteen, and a woman! And accordingly, thirty pages only further on, Ántonia dons a cook's apron at the Harlings in Black Hawk—a more feminine occupation that, the tempter ingratiatingly observes! And a pretty picture she makes, standing before a mixing-bowl in her tidy apron . . . But where is the *real* Ántonia?

Perhaps I have exaggerated the part which affection for her heroine[3] had in inducing Willa Cather to take Ántonia to the town. Yet who will say that sentimentality had no part in the sudden decision that took Ántonia from the plough? A sentimentality against which Willa Cather was all the less on her guard as it probably came to her dressed in the garb of that very realism, that same close adherence to her own experience which, in *O Pioneers*, had saved her from both unreality and sentimentality.[4] Realism, Willa Cather had not experienced yet, is a double-edged tool. A necessity in a novel which purports to represent a country and people which have played an important part in the writer's life, it should yet be kept a servant. Did Willa Cather sufficiently realize that realism and truth are not interchangeable terms? Patiently following Ántonia Shimerda's actual progress from care-free little girl to plodding farm-hand, from farm-hand to hired girl, and hired girl to wife and mother, Willa Cather neglected her artist's privilege, and duty, to excise, condense, select. The woman in her could care for Ántonia the hired girl as much as for Ántonia the farm girl; the artist should have seen that only the latter mattered, that the cook's apron hid where the farmer's

masculine garb revealed the essential, the deeper
Ántonia . . .

In *O Pioneers*, and still more in *The Song of the Lark*,
Willa Cather while controlling imagination by experience
had kept experience subservient to passion, the latter
book indeed deserving to be called, in Stuart Sherman's
eloquent words, "Miss Cather's most intimate book—the
book which she has most enriched with the poetry and
wisdom and passion of her experience, and made spacious
with the height and the depth of her desire."[5] Where *The
Song of the Lark* soared, *My Ántonia* kept close to the
solid earth, which gave it its strength, preserved it from
its predecessor's worst failures, yet left it, artistically,
an inferior book, one that, however rich with experience,
has not been made spacious with desire.[6]

VII

THERE are eight stories in *Youth and the Bright
Medusa* (1920), four old (*Paul's Case, A Wagner
Matinée, The Sculptor's Funeral, A Death in the Desert*)
and four new (*Coming, Aphrodite! The Diamond Mine,
A Gold Slipper, Scandal*), the essential difference between
earlier and later stories being that in the latter the stress
is more on the positive elements even in lives embittered
by pettiness, incomprehension and greed, hence a warmth,
fulness and balance lacking in *The Troll Garden* and
characteristic of Willa Cather's best work.

The new stories are all portraits of artists: a painter,
three operatic singers.

The painter (*Coming, Aphrodite!*) stands apart,[1] an
independent, rather surly young man, an experimenter,
a pupil of Cézanne, and "chiefly occupied with getting rid
of ideas he had once thought very fine" (18). The story
is of the sudden intrusion of woman into his life, woman
as represented by Eden Bower, a beautiful, superficial,
ambitious girl studying for the opera. A brief conjunction, then they fall apart, each following his and her own
destiny. The subject is commonplace enough, but Willa
Cather's art redeems it, saving it from insignificance by
touches of irony and tenderness, and a wise, contempla-
tive comprehension of the weakness of strong natures
when they first feel the urge of the flesh, the strength
of superficial natures when they feel themselves the targets
of desire.

The heroine of the next story, *The Diamond Mine*, is
an American prima donna, one of those buoyant personalities who hold irresistible fascination for crowds of
weaker natures, dilettantes, lovers, parasites, who live on

their strength, and, too often, on their purses, and scamper to another "diamond mine" when they have utterly exhausted the first. Not unlike *A Lost Lady* in its technique, *The Diamond Mine* begins with a portrait of the singer at the height of her power, reveals in sharp little vignettes the essential passages of her past, and ends on the grimly ironic picture of the shameless scramble for her property after her death on the *Titanic*. The story is perhaps the best in the book, a masterpiece of mingled irony and pathos, and a very lifelike portrait of one of those "generous, credulous creatures" (88) who are the salt of Willa Cather's world.

The other two stories are vindications of the artist, underlining the contrast between his actual life and the public's false, romantic idea of it.

" 'You are all,' (says Marshall McKann, the coal merchant to Kitty Ayrshire, the singer) 'you are all,' he went on steadily, watching her with indulgence, 'fed on hectic emotions. You are pampered. You don't help to carry the burdens of the world. You are self-indulgent and appetent.'

"(Answers Kitty Ayrshire): 'One should give pleasure to others . . . One should help others who are less fortunate . . . One should make personal sacrifices. I do; I give money and time and effort . . . Oh, I give something much more than that! something that you probably have never given to any one. I give, to the really gifted ones, my *wish*, my desire, my light, if I have any; and that, Mr. Worldly Wiseman, is like giving one's blood! . . . If you saw the houses I keep up,' she sighed, 'and the people I employ, and the motor-cars I run—And, after all, I've only this to do it with.' She indicated her slender person, which Marshall could almost have broken in two with his bare hands."[2]

Not *Scandal* or *A Gold Slipper* alone, the whole book might well be called a plea for a more intelligent, more sympathetic understanding of the artist's position, a more generous appreciation of all that he gives to the world.

" 'Your morality,' (Kitty Ayrshire says to Mc-Kann) 'seems to me the compromise of cowardice, apologetic and sneaking. When righteousness becomes alive and burning, you hate it as much as you do beauty. You want a little of each in your life, per-haps—adulterated, sterilized, with the sting taken out . . .' "[3]

—"Your morality," Willa Cather says to America in her next work, "is a lifeless business proposition. Beware lest it blight, not American art alone, but American youth."

VIII

ONE OF OURS (1922) is one of Willa Cather's four greatest books.[1] It is also, with *Death Comes for the Archbishop*, the one with the greatest unity of tone.

Willa Cather's characters had been simple, single-minded personalities, their problems chiefly problems of overcoming material difficulties: in *One of Ours* for the first time she portrays a complex figure's slow unfolding in time, for the first time (if we except the lifeless hero of *Alexander's Bridge*) her hero is divided against himself, his problem is the delicate one of adjustment to his milieu and to life, the finding of an ideal to which he can give himself.[2] The hero is Claude Wheeler, a Nebraskan farmer's son, the story that of his short life, from the fermentation of his adolescence on, through doubt and suffering, to the fulfilment of his hope, sacrifice of his life on the battlefield. That the sacrifice is made on foreign soil (Claude dies in the Argonne in 1918) and for a foreign faith (French civilization and culture, the French belief in the preëminence of ideas and feelings over material interests) implies a criticism of American materialism and American life all the more scathing as it is hardly ever more than implied.[3]

One of Ours may not be absolutely faultless (the last one hundred and fifty pages, however powerful—it is almost incredible that a woman could achieve such a stark picture of the horrors of the war—have less density than those before, they will age a little more rapidly), yet it is the best book Willa Cather had written so far. Compared to its predecessors, it goes deeper, it is richer in fine touches of observation and imagination, and, though far more complex, it is perfectly focused. Reading it is like reading *The Dead Souls, War and Peace* or *Sergeant*

Grischa. From the first page the discerning and delighted reader marks everywhere "the signs of genius at its task, absorbed and happy, haughty in its sweeping gestures, careless of our presence, bringing things to pass out of what seems nothing in particular, throwing about irrelevancies which grow into significance as we stare in perplexity."[4] The characters are little analyzed. What analysis is required when they stand revealed in dialogue and in action? Willa Cather is equally chary of descriptions—one touch, carefully selected, is enough to make the reader see a man, an incident, a landscape. You can trust his imagination to complete the picture you suggest.[5] The reader feels safe at last in Willa Cather's hands. The center of interest will not this time be suddenly shifted, nor the hero suddenly be dropped for somebody we care nothing about. So he gives himself to unmixed enjoyment of the book, delighting in that sane, comprehensive view of the world which gives it the force of an unprejudiced record.[6]

"The signs of genius at its task." Nowhere are they more evident than in the portrait of the Wheeler family with which the book opens, a portrait so fresh and unforgettable and true as to irresistibly recall that of the Tulliver family. The Wheelers stand on a background of pastures and cornland, around them the big, prosperous, disorderly farm on Lovely Creek. Mr. Wheeler the father, a florid personality, full of vitality and fun, liberal of his time and his money, always ready to attend to anybody's business but his own, a perfect egoist withal, utterly disregardful of other people's feelings—"a jolly, easy-going father indeed, for a boy who was not thin-skinned" (9). Mrs. Wheeler a retiring diffident soul, pious and sensitive, ignorant of life and afraid of the world, gladly confining herself to the narrow circle of her family and, except when Claude's interests and feelings are concerned, withdrawing into a spiritual world where everything is order and peace . . . Claude is the only one of her sons she feels any anxiety for. The other two are only too much at home in this hard world—Ralph, the youngest, because he has his father's perfect assurance and simple-hearted enjoyment of life and of his own little jokes; Bayliss, the eldest, because his is the positive, one-track mind that succeeds in the race for money and power. He would indeed succeed on a larger theater than Frankfort, where he has a prosperous farm-implement business, were he not a ruthless fanatic, handicapped and soured by dyspepsy, inclined to "regulate everybody's diet by his own feeble constitution" (8), afraid of stimulants and of unsterilized products (and ideas) of all kinds. Mahailey, the old servant, an illiterate "poor white," and a very simple soul, completes the family circle. Her head is full of crazy, half-formed ideas and suspicions, yet she is "shrewd in her estimate of people," quick to sense "all the shades of personal feeling, the accords and antipathies in the household" (20).

Claude stands among them, bullied by his father, who misses no occasion to trample on his son's pride, pitied though not always comprehended by his mother, petted by old Mahailey. With Ralph he gets on fairly well. Between Bayliss and him there is no love lost. He has one or two staunch friends outside of his family, yet he is terribly alone. His father's restlessness, his mother's sensitiveness combine in him to pull him "in two or three ways at once" (12). He has a splendid physique (which he takes for granted), red hair and a big head (which he is ashamed of), an inborn love of order, a keen sense of values and potentialities which makes his father's and Ralph's prodigality and carelessness as distasteful to him as Bayliss's exclusive pursuit of money. He is all ardent impulses for which neither farm work nor school work provide a sufficient outlet. He has an instinctive, urgent need to revere, but he will not bow to a low ideal.

We first see him at twenty or so, preparing "to go back to the struggling denominational college on the out-

skirts of the state capital, where he had already spent
two dreary and unprofitable winters" (21). Why does he
go back? His critical, clear-headed intelligence has long
since seen through his teachers, seen that, like their
worthy colleagues in *Elmer Gantry*, they are only
"preachers who couldn't make a living at preaching"
(21).[7] He does not really want to go back: he despises his
teachers, dismisses "all Christian theology as something
too full of evasions and sophistries to be reasoned about"
(42), and is equally contemptuous of his fellow students'
soppy way "of meekly accepting permitted pleasures"
(41).

He goes back, because, for all his clear independent
thinking and his violent temper, he cannot assert himself
against his family; because, as soon as he drops a hint of
wanting to go to the state university instead of to the
Temple, his father begins to banter him and he cannot
stand his father's pokes, his mother looks aggrieved
("Brother Weldon said many of the professors at the
state university are not Christian men")[8] and Claude
never wants to hurt that childlike faith of hers.

"Claude is on his way back to Lincoln, with a
fairly liberal allowance which does not contribute
much to his comfort or pleasure. He has no friends
or instructors whom he can regard with admiration,
though the need to admire is just now uppermost in
his nature. He is convinced that the people who might
mean something to him will always misjudge him and
pass him by. He is not so much afraid of loneliness
as he is of accepting cheap substitutes; of making
excuses to himself for a teacher who flatters him, of
waking up some morning to find himself admiring a
girl merely because she is accessible. He has a dread
of easy compromises, and he is terribly afraid of
being fooled" (29).

There are two oases in his dreary college life. He attends a seminar course in history at the university (for the first time he was encouraged to think, "for the first time he was studying a subject which seemed to him vital" (32)). He forms a friendship with the Erlichs, a German family.

At the Erlichs, in a sympathetic atmosphere of music, tobacco smoke, and lively conversation, Claude discovers new possibilities in family life and a higher way of living.

"He had never heard a family talk so much, or with anything like so much zest. Here there was none of the poisonous reticence he had always associated with family gatherings, nor the awkwardness of people sitting with their hands in their lap, facing each other, each one guarding his secret or his suspicion, while he hunted for a safe subject to talk about . . .

"Almost without realizing what he was doing, he tried to think things out and to justify his opinions to himself, so that he would have something to say when the Erlich boys questioned him. He had grown up with the conviction that it was beneath his dignity to explain himself, just as it was to dress carefully, or to be caught taking pains about anything . . . It wasn't American to explain yourself; you didn't have to! . . . If you got too much bored, you went to town and bought something new" (35, 37).

Here, he finds, are people who know how to live, people "who spend their money on themselves, instead of on machines to do the work and machines to entertain people" (36).

No sooner, however, has Claude been allowed to breathe the lighter, more congenial air of learning and of culture, than he must go back to the farm for good. A typically arbitrary decision of his father's entrusts him with the full responsibility of the farm, a huge affair, while Mr.

Wheeler, never loath to give himself a holiday, goes to settle Ralph on a ranch in Colorado.

It is hard on Claude. He who, only a few months earlier, stumblingly said to a friend: "Well, if we've only got once to live, it seems like there ought to be something—well, something splendid about life, sometimes" (44), now "flung himself upon the land and planted it with what was fermenting in him, glad to be so tired at night that he could not think" (66).

Days and weeks pass. Claude with characteristic faithfulness and *amour-propre* takes his work and his responsibilities much to heart (too much to heart as he shows when an accident for which he is not responsible depresses and humiliates him). He fails to find peace.

Work is all very well, but what is he working for? His father does not really care how he does the work, or even whether he does it at all.

Money? "He could not see the use of working for money, when money brought nothing one wanted."

Security? "To be assured, at his age, of three meals a day and plenty of sleep, was like being assured of a decent burial" (86).

In vain does he attempt "to subdue his own nature."

"When he thought he had at last got himself in hand, a moment would undo the work of days; in a flash he would be transformed from a wooden post into a living boy. He would spring to his feet, turn over quickly in bed, or stop short in his walk, because the old belief flashed up in him with an intense kind of hope, an intense kind of pain—the conviction that there was something splendid about life, if he could but find it!" (87).

A visit at the Erlichs makes him feel he does not belong there. He tries traveling. In vain. What's the use of

wandering where one feels "unrelated to anything" (99),
where one matters to no one? He goes back to the farm.
What else is there he *can* do? Again he works himself to
death, he tries not to think nor to dream. Life, he thinks
with the grim finality of twenty, has no more in store for
him than the same dull round of work, sleep, work, and
pleasures that do not satisfy. As he thus suffers and tor-
ments himself, love comes, and takes him by surprise.

Claude has no sisters. Girls, he has fought shy of,
ashamed of his awkwardness, his red hair and his freckles.
Women for him are sanctified beings, living, like his
mother, in a sphere apart, far above the grosser world
of men. No wonder then if, of the two girls he knows,
classmates and neighbors of his, an accident aiding he
chooses the wrong one. Gladys Farmer is the woman for
him, ardent, intelligent, free from small-town prejudice,
passionately fond of music . . . He must needs become
engaged to Enid Royce, a narrow, cold, puritanic nature
whose interests are impersonal and immaterial, an iron
will in a prim, frail-looking body. He sees only her grace-
fulness, feels unworthy of her, grateful for her patience
and kindness to him as he lies on a sick bed, his soul
aglow with admiration, humility and love. Her stubbornness, of which he has more than a glimpse, makes a charming contrast with her graceful appearance. Her very
passivity in his embrace, though it hurts him, he must
fain call the reserve of a pure nature.

"She would be slow to feel even a little of what he
was feeling; he knew that. It would take a long while.
But he would be infinitely patient, infinitely tender
for her . . . Even in his dreams he never wakened
her, but loved her while she was still and unconscious
like a statue. He would shed love upon her until she
warmed and changed without knowing why . . .
(120).

"He believed in the transforming power of marriage" (146).

The awakening is painful and swift. This is his bridal night:

"The train left Frankfort. He made his way through the aisles of swaying green curtains, and tapped at the door of his state room. It opened a little way, and Enid stood there in a white silk dressing-gown with many ruffles, her hair in two smooth braids over her shoulders.

" 'Claude,' she said in a low voice, 'would you mind getting a berth somewhere out in the car to-night? The porter says they are not all taken. I'm not feeling very well. I think the dressing on the chicken-salad must have been too rich.'

"He answered mechanically. 'Yes, certainly. Can't I get you something?'

" 'No, thank you. Sleep will do me more good than anything else. Good-night.'

"She closed the door and he heard the lock slip . . . (160).

. . . .

"By morning the storm of anger, disappointment, and humiliation that was boiling in him when he first sat down in the observation car, had died out. One thing lingered; the peculiarly casual, indifferent, uninterested tone of his wife's voice when she sent him away. It was the flat tone in which people make commonplace remarks about common things . . ." (161).

But why had Enid married him? Because, in her cool sexless way,[9] she is fond of Claude, proud of his strength, "solicitous for his comfort" (172). Because, when a woman has prohibition and foreign missions at heart, marriage enables her to do more for the good cause. Because, by marrying Claude, she hopes to reclaim him for the church . . . She is as much disappointed in him as he is in her. Claude flatly refuses to have anything to do with prohibition, foreign missions and the church, she seems to have offended him though she can't for the life of her see how, he has "moods of desperate silence" (173), he avoids her presence more and more. Claude meanwhile goes about his work, mechanically making the right gestures, feeling entrapped, hating himself "for accepting at all her grudging hospitality. He was wronging something in himself" (173).

His deliverance is nearer than he knows. Enid's sister falls ill in China, Enid calmly informs her husband that she is going over to nurse her. ("It isn't as if you couldn't be perfectly comfortable at your mother's . . . You mustn't be selfish," she says in substance to Claude).

"Claude knew that tone. Enid never questioned the rightness of her own decisions. When she made up her mind, there was no turning her. He went down the path to the barn with his hands stuffed in his trousers pockets, his bright pail hanging on his arm. Try again—what was there to try? Platitudes, littleness, falseness. . . . His life was choking him, and he hadn't the courage to break with it. Let her go! Let her go when she would! . . . What a hideous world to be born into! Or was it hideous only for him? Everything he touched went wrong under his hand—always had" (181).

Enid gone, Claude moves over to his mother's. His position he feels more absurd and hopeless than ever. One thing draws him out of himself and brings him nearer to his mother: his growing interest in the war news.[10]

At first the war means nothing to the Wheelers. European feuds are obscure and far away, Luxemburg and

Serbia but names on a map, names not so easily located either. Of France they know nothing, except that Paris is the wicked capital of pleasure, and the French are corrupt and pagan. The Germans are pacifists, idealists, and a splendid hard-working people. Gradually however, as the dramatic news pile on—Belgium invaded, Paris threatened, the French government removed to Bordeaux, the German invasion miraculously arrested at the Marne —Claude and his mother (they have become experts in map-reading now and pore over the encyclopaedia) begin to see a meaning in it all. It vitally matters to the world whether France goes down and brutal strength prevails. At first Claude's private tragedy made him forget the huge drama that was affecting millions of lives. Only as his wife leaves him and he lives again with his mother does he awaken to the consciousness of the greater misery of the world. The week before Christmas his wife left him. In April (1917) Claude starts for the training camp.

He does not feel he is doing anything unusual or meritorious: it is very little for a man to do. At least he is giving himself, a willing body and a ready mind, to help and save the country and the city which, whatever the rights or wrongs of their cause, are now threatened with annihilation.

The end is soon told. Claude goes over as a lieutenant with the A.E.F., volunteers all, boys going to the war in a spirit of brave adventure, giving a chivalrous answer to the call of a country of which most of them know nothing except that it needs them. He is happy at last. "Something was released that had been struggling for a long while, he told himself. He had been due in France since the first battle of the Marne; he had followed false leads and lost precious time and seen misery enough, but he was on the right road at last . . . (253) . . . The feeling of purpose, of fateful purpose, was strong in his breast" (254). Nothing can upset him now. Through the horrors of the passage across (a deadly epidemic breaks out on the crowded, old transport ship), the first estrangement in France,[11] the constant tension and precariousness of life at the front and the hell of battle, Claude carries a serene heart. Listening to the sound of the guns brings sweet assurance. "Men could still die for an idea; and would burn all they had made to keep their dreams . . . Ideals were not archaic things, beautiful and impotent; they were the real sources of power among men" (341).

And so it is a man at peace with the world and with himself, master of himself and of his men, who dies one September morning, feeling "only one thing; that he commanded wonderful men" (367).

"When [Mrs. Wheeler] can see nothing that has come of it all but evil, she reads Claude's letters over again and reassures herself; for him the call was clear, the cause was glorious. Never a doubt stained his bright faith. She divines so much that he did not write. She knows what to read into those short flashes of enthusiasm; how fully he must have found his life before he could let himself go so far—he, who was so afraid of being fooled! He died believing his own country better than it is, and France better than any country can ever be. And those were beautiful beliefs to die with. Perhaps it was as well to see that vision, and then to see no more. She would have dreaded the awakening—she sometimes even doubts whether he could have borne at all that last, desolating disappointment. One by one the heroes of that war . . . quietly die by their own hand . . . When Claude's mother hears of these things, she shudders and presses her hands tight over her breast, as if she had him there. She feels as if God had saved him from some horrible suffering, some horrible end. For as she reads, she thinks those slayers of themselves

were all so like him; they were the ones who had
hoped extravagantly—who in order to do what
they did had to hope extravagantly, and to believe
passionately. And they found they had hoped and
believed too much. But one she knew, who could ill
bear disillusion . . . safe, safe.

"Mahailey, when they are alone, sometimes ad-
dresses Mrs. Wheeler as 'Mudder'; 'Now, Mudder,
you go upstairs an' lay down an' rest yourself.'
Mrs. Wheeler knows that then she is thinking of
Claude, is speaking for Claude. As they are working
at the table or bending over the oven, something re-
minds them of him, and they think of him together,
like one person: Mahailey will pat her back and say,
'Never you mind, Mudder; you'll see your boy up
yonder.' Mrs. Wheeler always feels that God is near
—but Mahailey is not troubled by any knowledge of
interstellar spaces, and for her He is nearer still—
directly overhead, not so very far above the kitchen
stove.

— The End —" (371-2)

I have not tried to give a complete analysis of *One of
Ours*. There is much more in it than I have shown. I have
said little or nothing of its merits as a war book, of its
qualities as a portrait of Nebraskan or French life, little
or nothing of its interesting secondary characters. I have
chosen to concentrate rather on the hero, one of Willa
Cather's outstanding creations and, if not a typical rep-
resentative of American youth (there are not many Claude
Wheelers in any generation), at least "one of ours" and
typical of youth's blunders and youth's illusions, youth's
generous ardor.

A very human figure indeed, with the ironic contrast
between his fiery, absolute idealism and his apparently
passive acceptance of a reality that sadly mocks his
dreams. There is the same flaw in him as in Hamlet,

the same lack of correspondence between the idea and the act. At all the critical junctures of his life, whenever there is a choice to be made—Temple College or the state university; the farmer's or the scholar's life; Enid or Gladys; marriage or the war—he chooses, not what his keen critical intelligence tells him he ought to choose, but what he knows to hold but little promise of happiness for him. Has he then a total lack of moral backbone? On the contrary, as his fortitude in adversity shows he has considerable will power. How then shall we account for his making such a bungle of his life? There is no one explanation (Claude is no one-piece figure like Ántonia), no single cause for his failure. He fails because of the presence in him of conflicting elements (diffidence, impulsivity, sensitiveness, pride, humility, etc.), each one in itself a valuable asset in other circumstances and a different milieu; elements beneficial even in their combination and opposition (it is a good thing, e.g., that impulsivity should be checked by humility); elements that prove fatal to Claude so long as they are not coördinated and controlled by one guiding purpose.

That the favorable conditions are realized late is not his fault so much as that of circumstances. Born in pioneer days, the magnitude and necessity of the task before him would have absorbed his energies and proved the unifying power needed to turn his qualities to account. Brought up in a cultivated environment, with early access to the accumulated wealth of the past, how valuable to Claude, a scientist or a historian, would those very qualities prove that are such a handicap to Claude, Farmer Wheeler's son! Even as Farmer Wheeler's son, let his father be but a little more encouraging, a little more comprehensive, how different, how happier would Claude's life have turned out . . .

As it is, Claude is born in a coarse environment in prosperous times: his acute perception of the differences between himself and his family, of the discrepancy between his ideal and the surrounding reality, his father's brutal jocularity turns into diffidence, and dread of ridicule, and Claude develops a characteristic inferiority complex. He cannot be happy, or usefully engaged, on the farm where he naturally belongs. And, as he soon discovers in his short intercourse with the Erlich family and the state university and in his unsuccessful attempt at traveling, he cannot be happy where he does not belong. The result is the tangle we know, prolonged by the irony of fate (best perceptible in his marriage) and by his own peasant slowness at seeing the only way of escape open to him. Thus he stands, a tragic because a divided figure, a pathetic and a lovable example of our greatness and our impotence.

IX

A LOST LADY (1923), if not one of Willa Cather's most important works—to *The Song of the Lark* or *One of Ours* it stands in the same relation as a cameo or a pastel to a fresco—is a charming book, minor art, but very good of its kind.

It is the portrait of a lady. As in *My Mortal Enemy*, its companion piece, the heroine is seen through the impressionable eyes of a youth who feels to the full the fascination of her effervescent personality, the delicate charm of her conversation and her manners, and to whom comes as a painful shock the sudden revelation that his goddess is human, alas, all too human. The lady is Marian Forrester, wife to Captain Forrester, a big railroad man in the days when the Burlington road was being built "over the sage brush and cattle country, and on up into the Black Hills." The story is a drama in two acts. The first tells of the Forresters' days of glory, the happy days when their big, unpretentious house somewhere between Omaha and Denver was filled with distinguished visitors, railroad directors and gentlemen ranchers, robust, hearty personalities all of them, full of vast dreams and a healthy appetite for life—men on a scale with the bigness of the prairie. There is lavish hospitality at the Forresters' house, Captain Forrester sitting massive and serene, his very presence (not unlike that elderly French lieutenant's in *Lord Jim*) giving dignity and substance to the scene, Mrs. Forrester, twenty-five years his junior, keeping a lively flow of conversation with her guests, her eyes sparkling and smiling, her beautiful garnet earrings gracefully swinging beside her thin cheeks.

The happy days however are soon over. The first act ends on a disenchanting note and a catastrophe—Niel

Herbert, Mrs. Forrester's youthful admirer, finds out by chance that she has a lover. This scene has the ironic brutality of Maupassant. A bank, where small depositors had put their money because Captain Forrester was president, collapses. Captain Forrester unhesitatingly sacrifices his fortune so that "not one of the depositors should lose a dollar" and, as he comes home after the stormy bank meeting, he has a stroke which leaves him a helpless invalid.

Two or three years pass. Captain Forrester has grown fatter and heavier, and more taciturn. Mrs. Forrester has aged rapidly. The lines about her mouth show the strain her life is now, with an invalid husband, no servants, an empty house. Harder blows soon come. Her lover marries, her husband dies. She changes deeply. "For years Niel . . . and all her friends had thought of the Captain as a drag upon his wife . . . But without him, she was like a ship without ballast, driven hither and thither by every wind. She was flighty and perverse. She seemed to have lost her faculty of discrimination; her power of easily and graciously keeping everyone in his proper place." She must have society around her, and love. She invites the young men of the town, awkward, uneducated youths whose only talk is of business and of their clothes. She presides over the dullest of dinners, silk dress, garnet earrings and all, but her eyes are "hollow with fatigue" and she uses up "all her vitality to electrify these heavy lads into speech." She gives herself to Ivy Peters, a young brute of a "go-getter," a shyster, and a cold mean unfeeling man whom, in Captain Forrester's days, she would not have deigned to notice.[1] Her own comedown is symbolical of a general degeneration.

This is the end of an era. Shyster and speculator are everywhere evicting the pioneer and the builder. "A generation of shrewd young men, trained to petty economies by hard times" has replaced the first settlers. "The Old West had been settled by dreamers, greathearted adven-

turers who were unpractical to the point of magnificence;
a courteous brotherhood, strong in attack but weak in
defence, who could conquer but could not hold. Now all
the vast territory they had won was to be at the mercy
of men like Ivy Peters, who had never dared anything,
never risked anything."

The curtain drops on Ivy Peters the happy proprietor
of the Forresters' house and a married man. Mrs. Forrester dies in the Argentine as the wife of a "rich, cranky
old Englishman," a ranchman whom she evidently married for his money.[2]

Not Willa Cather's most important book, nor her most
perfect[3] (Mrs. Forrester is rather presented from the
outside than recreated from within, her story lacks the
copiousness and intimacy and warmth of Claude Wheeler's or Thea Kronborg's). *A Lost Lady* yet deserves high
praise. It is an accomplished portrait, a masterpiece of
concise narrative where every stroke tells, a dramatic
moving story whose "haunting loveliness lingers in the
mind afterwards with the delicacy of music,"[4] and leaves
behind a feeling of subtle pathos such as made Wordsworth exclaim:

Men are we, and must grieve when even the Shade
Of that which once was great is pass'd away.

X

THE story, in *The Professor's House* (1925), is of the slightest. Through casual (apparently casual) touches we learn to know Prof. St. Peter much as we would in real life—adding what we learn about him to-day to what we knew of him yesterday. He is fifty-two, a European history professor in a state university somewhere near Lake Michigan. He has just built a new house; he has two daughters, both happily married; he is very fond of gardening and extremely successful at it. His large, comfortable first-floor study is only a sham. The only place where he can work is an uncomfortable garret room on the third floor of the old house, a bare cold den he shares with Augusta the sewing woman, her patterns and "forms."

We see him move about the old study, thinking of the many entranced hours he spent there when, lost to the world, he was writing his *Spanish Adventurers in America*, the great work of his life. We watch him at the dinner table in the new house (he has built it with the £5000 Oxford prize his book has brought him), a handsome man in his well-cut dinner jacket, sarcastic or taciturn, evidently not quite at home in his new surroundings. We overhear a talk with his senior students, an animated, critical, man-to-man discussion of what science has given to the world. On a golden September afternoon with powerful over-arm stroke he swims in Lake Michigan, his arms and back "a deep terra cotta from a summer in the lake," his vermilion visor making his head look "sheathed and small and intensely alive, like the heads of the warriors on the Parthenon frieze in their tight, archaic helmets" (71).

Nothing much happens to Prof. St. Peter. He keeps

the old house for the sake of working and "reminiscing"
in the abandoned sewing-room. He gives some lectures in
Chicago, and he very nearly dies asphyxiated one stormy
night, for, as he lies on the couch in the old study, the
wind shuts the one small window to and the rusty gas
stove goes out. Nothing much happens, yet a mood is
achieved, an autumnal mood—fruition, fulfilment and a
bereavement, one's life work splendidly accomplished, one's
life strangely barer now, oneself unaccountably shy of
new contacts, unaccountably tired of the old ones. Looking back, Prof. St. Peter recaptures the ardor of the
days that are past, the happy days when "he had burned
his candle at both ends" (28), giving himself with the
same apparently inexhaustible energy to his wife and
daughters, to his garden and his students, to the great
book forever associated in his mind with the memory of
two vacations, the vision of two widely different yet
equally vivid landscapes. One was a blue mesa in New
Mexico, four-square and massive, "blue and purple rocks
and yellow-green piñons with flat tops, little clustered
[Cliff-Dweller] houses clinging together for protection, a
rude tower rising in their midst, rising strong, with calm-
ness and courage—behind it a dark grotto, in its depths
a crystal spring" (252-3); the other, the purple Medi-
terranean, a little Provençal brig, manned with lean
tawny seamen, riding low on it, the professor dreamily
watching from its deck "snow peak after snow peak" of
the Sierra Nevada tower above him, "high beyond the
flight of fancy . . . : and the design of his book un-
folded in the air above him, just as definitely as the mountain ranges themselves. And the design was sound. He
had accepted it as inevitable, had never meddled with it,
and it had seen him through" (106).

Those were the days . . . His two daughters' pretty
frocks gaily flashed through the house. His wife kept
unobtrusive order and gave taste and dignity to their
life. *The Spanish Adventurers* was slowly, irresistibly

taking shape, and one responsive, eager-eyed student more than repaid the professor for a thousand dull ones. *Tempi passati* . . . The little girls are married women. Money has hardened one; lack of money, and consequent jealousy of her sister, embittered the other. Mrs. St. Peter, still a handsome woman, knows a kind of an Indian summer, not altogether to the professor's taste, basking, as uncritically, unashamedly as ever Queen Victoria drinking in Disraeli's florid praise, in the sincere though rather excessive adoration of young Marsellus, her favorite son-in-law, a gallant young Semite. Money has not corrupted the professor, but it has come between him and the friends of his youth, stirring up envy and spite around him. Tom Outland, his best student, and, ironically enough, the posthumous cause of Marsellus's and Rosamond's wealth, has died, a volunteer, in the war . . .

This is the autumn of a well-filled life, melancholy spreading a gradual veil over the passions of the spring and the summer that are no more, disenchantment growing, and an ever-stronger need of retiring into oneself, of going back, purged of intellect and sex, to the boy one was at first, the primitive who was "only interested in earth and woods and water." "He found he could lie on his sand-pit by the lake for hours and watch the seven motionless pines drink up the sun. In the evening, after dinner, he could sit idle and watch the stars, with the same immobility. . . . He seemed to know, among other things, that he was solitary and must always be so; he had never married, never been a father. He was earth, and would return to earth. When white clouds blew over the lake like bellying sails, when the seven pine trees turned red in the declining sun, he felt satisfaction and said to himself merely, 'That is right.' Coming upon a curly root that thrust itself across his path, he said, 'That is it.' When the maple leaves along the street began to turn yellow and waxy, and were soft to the touch—

like the skin on old faces—he said, 'That is true; it is time.' All these recognitions gave him a kind of sad pleasure" (263-6).

Youth's eager conquest of life, maturity's calm dominion over it, age's dispassionate acceptance of nature's ways and of the inevitable end, they are all in *The Professor's House*, all felt by one man, *lived* by him. An ideal figure? An idealized one rather,[1] handsomer, more superbly, harmoniously alive than most of us, a brother to Milton's Adam or Durer's, yet one of us all the same. "One of ours," he, too, a man very definitely located in space and time, an American of typically mixed origins,[2] stubbornly fighting for clear independent thinking in a university where the higher values are constantly threatened by commercialism and conformity.[3] A very human figure is Prof. St. Peter, a scholar devoid of pedantry, a *savant* not divorced from life, an intellectual who is also a man of action, a sportsman, an artist and a gourmet.

There are other interesting characters in *The Professor's House*. Mrs. St. Peter, a blonde beauty, her face and character both a trifle harder than the delicate tints of her complexion and the smiling radiance of her eyes would first make you think. Rosamond, the elder daughter, a strikingly handsome brunette, whose commanding beauty easily makes all men (all but her very critical father and her superbly generous husband) blind to the slight imperfections of her physique, the limitations of her intelligence and the essentially hard core of her personality, and her careless disregard of other people's feelings. Her sister, Kathleen, an altogether different personality: a pale, slender girl, with a charming, intelligent face, a "spirited tilt of her head" (37), and too much sensitiveness, and too much pride, not to find life a little more cruel than she should.[4] Tom Outland; his friend Rodney Blake; Augusta the seamstress, "a reliable, methodical spinster, a German Catholic and very devout" (16), young Marsellus, Rosamond's husband, a living, fascinating exemplar of that curious flexibility of backbone which makes the men of his race impervious to rebuff and, usurers or saints, tenacious as Gentiles never are . . . They are all living men and women, built with short, cumulative touches, presented with that calm impartiality which we have come to look for in Willa Cather's books.[5] Men and women engaged, like the professor himself, in that same implacable process of growing, loving, suffering, hardening which only ends with life. Knowing but troubled moments of happiness, unless, like Augusta the seamstress, or the Professor himself in the end, they learn "to live without delight" (282) and accept the hardest facts of life as inevitable realities, neither good nor bad.

The book, from its quiet opening[6] on to its quiet end, is a masterpiece of unity of tone and novel, unobtrusive composition. No slow unfolding in time here but a deep, comprehensive cut into the professor's life as he stands on the threshold of old age. Excursions back into his past as he now pensively, now serenely, recalls this or that episode of it. One excursion, *Tom Outland's Story*, longer than the others, stretches over one-fourth of the book and takes us back not to the professor's own past but to his favorite pupil's, when, a poor callboy and cowpuncher, he discovered and studied and loved a Cliff Dweller city in the heart of an unexplored mesa. The length of the episode, its sudden shifting of the interest from the professor's story to Tom Outland's, may be resented at first. It does not take long, I think, to perceive that the episode, while seemingly breaking the structural unity of the book, in fact strengthens it, enriches it, rounding off, as it does, the professor's portrait, making us acquainted with the Tom Outland in him, the adventurer, the explorer and resuscitator of the past, the man in love with the obscure, the beautifully human origins of the race, that first "hardest of all starts" (221) when men lifted themselves from brutality to organized existence, security and the arts of peace.

"The best form is that which makes the most of its subject."[7] We may very well conceive of *The Professor's House* built along more traditional lines, but we cannot imagine a more traditional form making more of the subject than the actual *Professor's House* does. For the book stands, a singularly moving creation, "a disturbingly beautiful" book,[8] a work of art with both the refinements of a subtle technique and the direct warmth of life. It is a masterpiece of comprehension, selection and restraint, with an atmosphere all its own yet typically "Willa Catherian" (typical of her later books), a tender, golden luminousness bathing landscape and man in the same autumnal pensiveness.

IN PERHAPS every writer's work there are books, written in the interval between two important works, which show a weakening of the author's grasp, betray a diminution of his creative strength. *My Mortal Enemy* (1926), sandwiched in between *The Professor's House* and *Death Comes for the Archbishop*, like *Paradise Regained* between *Paradise Lost* and *Samson Agonistes*, seems to me such a book.

Like *A Lost Lady*, which it strikingly resembles in several respects, though it is inferior to it, *My Mortal Enemy* is a story of a woman's decline told as a drama in two acts.

The first shows Myra Henshawe, a brilliant, ambitious woman, at the zenith of her worldly success, the center and pivot of a distinguished New York coterie. They are people for whom she can never do enough, but whom, if we interpret correctly what little Willa Cather tells us about her, she would fain reduce to an exclusive dependence on her as Proust's Mme. Verdurin or Julien Green's Mme. Londe had brought *their* little circles. She is not perfectly happy. Little things, like having to hire a hansom when she wants to drive round Central Park, cause her secret discontent, but at least she enjoys to the full the gratifying sense of her power over her dependents and admirers, the most devoted of whom is her husband. When the second act opens a double catastrophe has taken place. Myra's husband, through no fault of his, has lost his well-paid job and is reduced to "shabby-genteel poverty";[1] Myra herself has been stricken in her health, she is an embittered, helpless invalid, unresigned to her fate, torturing her husband and herself with constant, fruitless imagination of the might-have-beens, mercilessly desecrating her happy past. "We were never really happy. . . . I was always a grasping worldly woman; I was never satisfied. . . . Perhaps I can't forgive him [her husband] for the harm I did him. . . ."

Here were all the elements of a great book: a pathetic story, a complex character, selfish and generous, ardent and tyrannical, the sufferings of thwarted passions and frustrated hopes. Unfortunately, not only does Willa Cather's delicate, pastel-like picture of New York—New York in the days when Sarah Bernhardt's *Hamlet* was the talk of the town—fail to make any lasting impression on the mind, but, for all its dramatic contrasts and arresting episodes, no sooner is the book closed than its contours are blurred and Myra Henshawe has faded into an insubstantial wraith.

Lack of analysis is responsible for this. Willa Cather, never an analyst, managed in *The Song of the Lark*, *One of Ours* and *A Lost Lady* to replace analysis by conversation and action, just as in *The Professor's House* she transmuted it into pensive reminiscence. In all four books the result was good: tell-tale dialogue, retrospection, and action, more than compensated for the absence of analysis. An abundance and precision of details, a crowd of striking characters surrounding the central figure helped to create, from the first page, a convincing impression of reality. In *My Mortal Enemy* on the contrary the dialogue is generally monologue, and not very personal monologue at that. Analysis there is none, and very little detail;[2] there is only one character that counts, Myra Henshawe herself.[3] A short series of incidents, characteristic episodes of Myra's life, serve to give us an impression of her personality and are all we have to form an idea of either her character or her life. The incidents are too few, they stand too far apart in time. They tell us too little; we feel too much at the mercy of an omniscient author who grudges us information or only seems willing to give it in the most desultory way. So the reader becomes discouraged, takes but a perfunctory interest in the book, leaves it unsatisfied and hastens to forget it.

He is right. Out of even such material as Willa Cather had in Myra Henshawe's story and with as few *dramatis personae* Benjamin Constant wrote *Adolphe*, Marcel Proust *Un Amour de Swann*, books where an exhaustive and merciless analysis gave permanent reality, and an almost unbearable pathos to the story of even such tortured souls as Myra—but how alive they!

XII

EXCEPTION has been taken to masterpieces like *The Song of the Lark* or *The Professor's House* on the score of faulty or loose composition. I can think of no fault that could reasonably be found with *Death Comes for the Archbishop* (1927), Willa Cather's latest book up to date, unless it be its misleading and rather cumbrous title, singularly inappropriate, with its bitter *Dance of Death* connotation, its suggestion of desperate struggle and sudden wrench from the joys of life, for a book full of serenity, the story not of violent death but of a consecrated life leading on to a peaceful end.[1]

Its composition is peculiar. Unlike the reminiscent meanderings of *The Professor's House*, the strict dramatic composition of the shorter novels, the straightforward narrative of *One of Ours* or *The Song of the Lark*, it might be called a return to the simple, undramatic method, the *pictorial* method, used in *My Ántonia*. A return triumphant, for, whereas *My Ántonia*, as I pointed out, was an imperfect work of art, completely lacking unity, *Death Comes* . . . is a masterpiece of construction, a succession of arresting episodes bound together by unity of place (New Mexico), of time (the 1850's) and of action (the spiritual conquest of their diocese by the first Catholic bishop and his coadjutor, the two principal characters of the book).

Willa Cather herself has told[2] how the work took shape in her mind. The idea first came to her in the course of her wanderings in the Southwest, the Southwest dear to her from her first sojourn there in 1912, the Southwest in whose clear glittering atmosphere she set Thea Kronborg's childhood and Tom Outland's *Wanderjahre*.

"The longer I stayed in the Southwest, the more I felt that the story of the Catholic Church in that country was the most interesting of all its stories. The old mission churches, even those which were abandoned and in ruins, had a moving reality about them; the hand-carved beams and joists, the utterly unconventional frescoes, the countless fanciful figures of the saints, no two of them alike, seemed a direct expression of some very real and lively human feeling. They were all fresh, individual, first-hand."[3]

"One traveled slowly, and had plenty of time for reflection." Listening to stories told her by old Mexicans, traders, and priests, Willa Cather imagined the country as it was in the early days of its acquisition by the Federal government when a few soldiers, traders, adventurers and priests were the only white inhabitants,[4] and Santa Fé, the only town, was "a thin, wavering adobe town" with a green plaza, one long street, and a tall church whose earthen towers "rose high above the flatness" in an amphitheatre of steep "carnelian-colored hills" (19).

The stories were of deaths in the desert, the cruelty of Indian raids, the heroism, fanaticism and greed of the first Spanish missionaries, the gentleness, sanctity, devotion and courage of the first Catholic bishop, a Frenchman by the name of Lamy. The stories meant much to Willa Cather—there was a quality of greatness about them, suggestive of no mean sufferings and no mean passions. They meant all the more to her now that she had intimate knowledge of the country, its beauty, its discomforts, its dangers.

In Willa Cather's mind there was no story as yet. A central figure was needed to crystallize the scattered elements reality offered. Bishop Lamy could have become that figure, but she knew too little about him. Only when she came across Father Howlett's life of Bishop Machebeuf (Father Lamy's close associate and friend, and the Father Joseph of her book) did she really *see* the man, the two men rather, for, side by side with Father Lamy stood Father Joseph Machebeuf, as inseparable from him, and as different, as Sancho from Don Quixote. Two men riding across the desert, braving storm, accident, hostility and drought, christening, marrying, forcing reluctant priests to obedience, reforming abuses, bringing everywhere through their immense, ill-defined diocese, to souls benighted, rude, yet not altogether oblivious of the true faith, the grace of culture, kind words and kind deeds.

Thus was *Death Comes for the Archbishop* born, Willa Cather's greatest book perhaps, not a novel so much as a chronicle, an imaginative, artistic reconstruction of events and men that, but for it, would be lost in obscure devotional books or left at the mercy of ever-shifting oral traditions.

"My book was a conjunction of the general and the particular, like most works of the imagination. I had all my life wanted to do something in the style of legend, which is absolutely the reverse of dramatic treatment. Since I first saw the Puvis de Chavannes frescoes of the life of Sainte Geneviève in my student days, I have wished that I could try something a little like that in prose; something without accent, with none of the artificial elements of composition. In the Golden Legend the martyrdoms of the saints are no more dwelt upon than are the trivial incidents of their lives; it is as though all human experiences, measured against one supreme spiritual experience, were of about the same importance. The essence of such writing is not to hold the note, not to use an incident for all there is in it—but to touch and pass on. I felt that such writing would be a kind of discipline in these days when the 'situation' is made to count for so much in writing . . . In this kind of writing the mood is the thing. . . . What I got from Father Machebeuf's letters was the mood, the spirit in which they accepted the accidents and hardships of a desert country, the joyful energy that kept them going. To attempt to convey this hardihood of spirit one must use language a little stiff, a little formal, one must not be afraid of the old trite phraseology of the frontier. Some of those time-worn phrases I used as the note from the piano by which the violinist tunes his instrument . . . I did not sit down to write the book until the feeling of it had so teased me that I could not get on with other things. The writing of it took only a few months, because the book had all been lived many times before it was written, and the happy mood in which I began it never paled. It was like going back and playing the early composers after a surfeit of modern music."[5]

The "discipline" paid. Having renounced all pretensions to drama, "situation," love interest, and all the other paraphernalia of fiction, and proposing to herself but little, Willa Cather achieved more than she proposed. Not a Puvis de Chavannes fresco. Her book, if it has the monumental quality of a fresco, has colors more intense than any Puvis de Chavannes used. Not another Golden Legend, for in the Golden Legend the sublime and the grotesque jostle each other. Whereas *Death* . . . for all its variety has perfect harmony of tone. Not a mere chronicle either. Willa Cather's story, however direct and simple, opens vistas into the remote past of the Spaniards, the remoter past of the Indians, spreads about boundless horizons, suggests subtle nuances of character, intimate speechless interchange of impressions and sympathies, all beyond the reach of even the best chronicler.

She achieved a unique book, at times reminding one of those intimate portraits of humble saintly lives which

Sainte-Beuve's careful hand painted in *Port-Royal*, at other times recovering the humor and gusto of Daudet's ecclesiastical stories[6] yet, in the end, only comparable to itself. An achievement all the more remarkable as this virile book is the work of a woman, this deeply Catholic book the work of a Protestant writer,[7] and one who has accomplished the *tour de force* of interesting even the most sophisticated reader in her simple account of the lives and personalities of two perfectly good and perfectly different men.

Much of the telling force of the book is due to Willa Cather's intense visualization of its characters and scenes, a visualization communicated to the reader by infallible choice of the characteristic detail and extreme felicity in the selection, arrangement and economy of words, all of which will be best illustrated by a few short quotations:

(thirsting mare scenting water): "All at once Father Latour thought he felt a change in the body of his mare. She lifted her head for the first time in a long while, *and seemed to redistribute her weight upon her legs*" (21).

(clouds): "Whether they were dark and full of violence, or soft and white with luxurious idleness, they powerfully affected the world beneath them. The desert, the mountains and mesas, were continually reformed and recolored by the cloud shadows. The whole country seemed fluid to the eye under this constant change of accent, this ever-varying distribution of light" (96-7).

(the desert): "Everything was dry, prickly, sharp; Spanish bayonet, juniper, greasewood, cactus; the lizard, the rattlesnake—and man made cruel by a cruel life" (279).

(an old man): "His right eye was overgrown by a cataract, and he kept his head tilted as if he were trying to see around it. *All his movements were to the left, as if he were reaching or walking about some obstacle in his path*" (85).

(the priest of Taos): "His broad high shoulders were like a bull buffalo's, his big head was set defiantly on a thick neck, and the full-cheeked, richly colored, egg-shaped Spanish face—how vividly the Bishop remembered that face! . . . His mouth was the very assertion of violent, uncurbed passions and tyrannical self-will; the full lips thrust out and taut, like the flesh of animals distended by fear or desire" (141).

(at the priest of Taos'): "As the night wind blew into the room, a little dark shadow fluttered from the wall across the floor; a mouse, perhaps. But no, it was a bunch of woman's hair that had been indolently tossed into a corner when some slovenly female toilet was made in this room. This discovery annoyed the Bishop exceedingly" (150).

(a dreadful warning): "Instantly that stupid face became intense, prophetic, full of awful meaning. With her finger she pointed them away, away!—two quick thrusts into the air. Then, with a look of horror beyond anything language could convey, *she threw back her head and drew the edge of her palm quickly across her distended throat*—and vanished. The doorway was empty; the two priests stood staring at it, speechless" (69).

This consummate art Willa Cather uses to impress upon us her vision of a landscape, its scattered inhabitants, and the two French priests bent upon their spiritual conquest.

The landscape we first see through the impression it makes on the young bishop, new to the country and astray in the strange, geometrical landscape.

"As far as he could see, on every side, the landscape was heaped up into monotonous red sand-hills, not much larger than haycocks, and very much the shape of haycocks. One could not have believed that in the number of square miles a man is able to sweep with the eye there could be so many uniform red hills . . . He must have traveled through thirty miles of these conical red hills, winding his way in the narrow cracks between them, and he had begun to think that he would never see anything else. They were so exactly like one another that he seemed to be wandering in some geometrical nightmare . . . Every conical hill was spotted with smaller cones of juniper, a uniform yellowish green, as the hills were a uniform red. The hills thrust out of the ground so thickly that they seemed to be pushing each other, elbowing each other aside, tipping each other over.

"The blunted pyramid, repeated so many hundred times upon his retina and crowding down upon him in the heat, had confused the traveler, who was sensitive to the shape of things.

"*'Mais, c'est fantastique!'* he muttered, closing his eyes to rest them from the intrusive omnipresence of the triangle" (14-5).

"Hundreds of square miles of thirsty desert, then a spring, a village, old men trying to remember their catechism to teach their grandchildren" (30). Such is the newly-formed apostolic vicarate, with its scattered inhabitants, humble Mexican settlers, simple and trusting, true Christians at heart for all their piety is melodramatic and crude, generous with the uncalculating generosity of the poor. Native priests, some, "simple almost to childishness" (85); others, Padre Lucero the miser, Padre Martinez the dissolute old priest of Taos,[8] corrupt and tyrannical; nomad Indians of the plains, dignified and mysterious, passing over the face of the land "without disturbing anything," ravaging "neither the rivers nor the forest, and if they irrigated [taking] as little water

as would serve their needs" (236-7) ; pueblo Indians, fixed
on their mesa tops from times immemorial, "increasing
neither in numbers nor desires, rock-turtles on their rock"
(104),—impervious to Christianity:

> "The Bishop . . . had never found it so hard to
> go through the ceremony of the Mass. Before him,
> on the grey floor, in the grey light, a group of bright
> shawls and blankets, some fifty or sixty silent faces;
> above and behind them the grey walls. He felt as if
> he were celebrating Mass at the bottom of the sea,
> for antediluvian creatures; for types of life so old,
> so hardened, so shut within their shells, that the sac-
> rifice on Calvary could hardly reach back so far.
> . . . When he blessed them and sent them away, it
> was with a sense of inadequacy and spiritual defeat.
> "Something reptilian he felt there,[9] something
> that had endured by immobility, a kind of life out
> of reach, like the crustaceans in their armor" (101-2,
> 104).

Again with a few firm strokes Willa Cather draws the
portraits of the two French priests: Bishop, later Archbishop Latour (the Father Lamy of history), and Father,
later Bishop Joseph Vaillant (Father Machebeuf),—an
immortal pair!

A picturesque, almost picaresque figure is Father Joseph, the baker's son of Riom.

> "The Lord had made few uglier men. He was short,
> skinny, bow-legged. . . . His skin was hardened and
> seamed by exposure to weather in a bitter climate,
> his neck scrawny and wrinkled like an old man's. A
> bold, blunt-tipped nose, positive chin, a very large
> mouth—the lips thick and succulent but never loose,
> never relaxed, always stiffened by effort or working
> with excitement. His hair, sunburned to the shade of

dry hay, had originally been tow-colored . . . Even
his eyes were nearsighted, and of such a pale, watery
blue as to be unimpressive" (37).

Within this frail, "poorly-built body" (Father Joseph
richly deserves his nickname of *Trompe-la-mort*), under
this unprepossessing envelope there is an iron fortitude,
the energy and "driving power of a dozen men" (37). His
appearance is slightly comical, his intellect, imagination
and faith are those of a child who interprets any happy
event as a direct intervention of providence, St. Joseph,
or the Blessed Virgin herself. He goes about dragging
after him a wallet chockfull of consecrated "crosses,
rosaries, prayer books, medals, breviaries" (231) and
other holy trash. Yet no man can resist him, nothing can
dampen his spirit, his naïve singleness of purpose, tanta-
mount to genius, wins the rich man's mules for the church
and despises not the poor man's humbler, more sponta-
neous gift. He amuses, refreshes, touches his bishop, who,
when he feels embarrassed by his friend's begging per-
tinacity or shocked at his fondness for good cuisine, re-
members that the man never asks anything for himself,
never complains "about the hardness and scantiness of
the fare on his long missionary journeys," and transforms
"into spiritual energy," a dinner that would make another man heavy.

"Though the Bishop had worked with Father Joseph
for twenty-five years now, he could not reconcile the con-
tradictions of his nature . . . Nothing one could say of
Father Vaillant explained him. The man was much greater
than the sum of his qualities" (228, 231).

Shoulder to shoulder with the gesticulating little man
stands the bishop, an Auvergnat like his vicar, a fellow
seminarian, yet an altogether different man. Intelligent
and handsome, calm and dignified, the distinguished son
of "an old family of scholars and professional men"
(225), this cultured aristocrat seems little fitted to live

the missionary's life and undergo its discomforts and its
hardships. His delicate sensibility,[10] his unfailing courtesy to man, woman and beast,[11] the native reserve which
makes it impossible for him to be hail-fellow-well-met with
the natives as Father Joseph so easily is, are heavy handi-
caps in a man who has to deal with primitive conditions
of life and rough, uneducated men. The bishop is still
further handicapped by being keenly conscious of his
deficiencies. He has moments of doubt, of spiritual
drought, moments when his ineffective words glide on the
Indians' hard carapace, and his work seems "superficial,
a house built upon the sands."

> "His great diocese was still a heathen country.
> The Indians traveled their old roads of fear and dark-
> ness, battling with evil omens and ancient shadows.
> The Mexicans were children who played with their
> religion" (212).

At such times nothing can help him like Father Joseph's companionship, the example of his fervor and his
zeal. They fill him with humiliation and admiration, renew his confidence in his mission and in its ultimate success. A success due no less to himself than to his vicar.
For the bishop has wonderful assets. To his vicar's energy
and resolution he adds perspicacity and intelligence. He
is a keen judge of events and of men. He knows when to
strike and when to temporize. He has authority and fore-
sight, sang-froid, and a love of order that, in a country
where "lawless personal power" (141) has been the rule,
is a civilizing, humanizing force. The very qualities which
seemed due to handicap him work in his favor. The reserve,
if it awes the Mexicans, wins him the Indians' regard and
their confidence. His sensibility and courteousness impress
the roughest brutes, not only because they are the natural expression of a superior nature but because they soon

prove to be but the smooth outer case of a fortitude and courage only equaled by his friend's.

The two priests' ends are in keeping with their respective natures. Father Joseph, as befits him, dies in the harness, a limping shriveled old man, lean and agile as a monkey, traveling "thousands of miles . . . among the mountain towns" (289) of Colorado, his new diocese. Father Latour peacefully ends his days in retirement, lovingly tending his beautiful fruit garden, giving instruction to the new priests from France, reading "St. Augustine, or the letters of Madame de Sévigné, or his favorite Pascal" (278), praying, meditating, "living over his life" (285).

His great work is accomplished. There is order in his diocese, and the cathedral he has built rises clear-cut and strong on a background of dark pines and carnelian-colored hills.

"When the Cathedral bell tolled just after dark, the Mexican population of Santa Fé fell upon their knees, and all American Catholics as well. Many others who did not kneel prayed in their hearts. Eusabio and the Tesuque boys went quietly away to tell their people; and the next morning the old Archbishop lay before the high altar in the church he had built. The End" (303).

Thus the great book comes to a close, its last words as eloquent in their restrained pathos as those simple, solemn words that end, on a note unemphatic and grave, the majestic harmonies of *Paradise Lost*.

XIII

WHAT works Willa Cather will yet give us it would be rash to say, for who, when *A Lost Lady* was her latest work, could have foreseen *The Professor's House*, or who, reading that in 1925, could have guessed that it would be followed in quick succession by books as different from each other and from it as *My Mortal Enemy* and *Death Comes for the Archbishop*? Safer, more profitable, however eagerly we may await her next book, to look back from the lofty altitudes of *Death Comes for the Archbishop* over the tract of ground that Willa Cather has conquered and made hers (and ours) for ever.

What progress from those early days when a young college girl was writing sentimental versions of pioneer life back in Nebraska!

Not a regular progress perhaps. The road that goes up from the college stories to *Death Comes for the Archbishop* has sudden ascents and no less sudden drops and long level stretches. Only with *O Pioneers* does it reach any high level. With *The Song of the Lark* it goes up to fall again; so does it, though both rise and fall are less, in *My Ántonia*. *One of Ours* is a high windy plateau; *A Lost Lady* one lower and less extensive. In *The Professor's House* we are on the heights again. We plunge down for a short interval (*My Mortal Enemy*) and once more, with *Death Comes for the Archbishop*, breathe the clean mountain air.

Not a regular progress—yet if we compare starting point and height of latest achievement, what an advance in range of observation and of feeling, flexibility of style, firmness and catholicity of character drawing, imaginative recasting or reality, ejection of sentimentality by classic restraint and steady-eyed contemplation of truth!

It all began with *O Pioneers*, itself made possible by those two far-reaching decisions of Willa Cather's: her wise resolve, after the false start of the college stories, to live before she wrote again, and her final resolution (*O Pioneers*) to leave off trying to "write well," to express, as simply and as truthfully as she could, what was deepest in her.

After *O Pioneers* there was still much to do, a last outgrowth of sentimentality to be weeded out, reality to be interpreted with more liberty, characters more intellectual and more complex to be portrayed, a more lifelike dialogue to be achieved, etc. Yet there was in it the germ of all the best she was to give to the world.

There was that intimate knowledge of a country which was then Nebraska only (modern Nebraska and the Nebraska of the pioneers) but was soon to stretch out in space and in time, gathering in Arizona, Colorado and New Mexico unto itself, reaching back to the first start of civilized existence in the ancient Cliff Cities. A knowledge of all the country's changes, aspects and moods, a knowledge at once panoramic and detailed, suffused with emotion, expressed with restrained lyric fervor.

There was a deep understanding of the problems and difficulties of the two generations of immigrants. The elder Bergsons and Lindstrums, handicapped by memories, old habits, disappointments and regrets; their sons and daughters, taking to the new country and to their work with a hungry appetite, turning the land's resistance into fruitfulness and plenty.

The spontaneity and warm passions of Latins and Slavs, German *Gemütlichkeit* and German music, French culture and French cuisine, the Mexicans' love of color and of music, Scandinavian stolidity and Scandinavian unrest, in *O Pioneers* and its successors Willa Cather was interested in all. Were they not all integral parts of a beautifully diversified world?

The pioneers had come to the West from over a continent and over the seas, driven on by sheer necessity, by hunger, greed, mad hopes. Driven on by their dreams. Dreams sordid or splendid—*dreams*, i.e., imagination, an emotion, sometimes an idea, the glamor of a new world of untold possibilities—man's eternal quest for the Garden of Eden, Eldorado, the Fountain of Youth.

When they had reached the promised land, and death had taken his toll of the weaker, stern necessity made most of the survivors forget that they had ever dreamed. Oscar, Amédée, Ambrosch sullenly or cheerfully drove the plough, Alexandra and Ántonia found in patient utilization of reality and (Ántonia at least) in maternity a sufficient outlet for their creative energies.

Side by side with these however, brothers to them, stood those very different figures, Emil Bergson, Carl Lindstrum, Claude Wheeler later on, the dissatisfied, the divided, the dreamers, youths who should have been born earlier, when the world was boundless and wild and there were still tasks asking for superhuman strength.

There were thus two principal types of characters in Willa Cather's early original work: the realists (Alexandra, Amédée, Thea, Ántonia), the adventurers (Emil, Carl, Claude Wheeler), the former generally being women, the latter men.[1]

Realist or adventurer, they were all young. Only as she herself advanced in years did she choose middle-aged men and women as protagonists of her stories; only from *A Lost Lady* onwards did she give any prominence to the problems, and the pathos, of the oncoming of age.

More complex and more subtly drawn, her later heroes were yet of the same race as her early ones. There was in them as solid a substratum of pioneer virtues and as potent a ferment of unrest. They united (the combination, not the elements, was new) the energy, obstinacy, adaptability to new circumstances that had been Alexandra's or Ántonia's, to Emil's or Claude's ferment of unrest. But the pioneer virtues they applied to conquests immaterial—the artist's conquest of his art and of himself, the priest's conquest of a country for God and the harder conquest of his own disappointments, repugnances and doubts. The unrest, which in Emil and Claude had resulted in aimless wandering and in misery (until one found peace in the very heart of passion and the other in the fiery furnace of a dreadful war), professor and priest, because they were strong enough to control it, direct it, subordinate it to a definite ideal, turned it to a blessing and made it creative.

To prevent sentimentality from flooding and distorting her work, Willa Cather first had recourse to silence and disguise (the silence of the first post-graduate years, the disguise of Jamesian analysis and Jamesian style). When she felt that she could throw off the mask, and step out as herself, she was still careful to keep her romantic characters more or less in the background, throwing the light of her art on those rather stern realists, her heroines. Only in *One of Ours* did she once more make a romantic youth the hero of one of her books.[2]

She could do it safely. She had a sufficient grasp of reality now to exorcise any potential sentimentality, or unreality, in the conception of a romantic hero.

And indeed, romantic though they may be (are not they too adventurers and dreamers at heart?), Claude Wheeler and her later heroes are real men, they live in a very real world, their feet firmly planted on solid western earth; their experience (secretly nourished by Willa Cather's) colored by their environment and influenced by it; their problems—not only the unusual problems (unusual because most men are content to live from day to day without asking questions) of finding a worthy reason

to live and, when they have found it, of living up to their
ideal, but the common, everyday problems which confront
every one of us. The money problem, the religious problem, the problem of marriage, the many delicate problems of adjustment to one's family, one's profession, one's
environment, adjustment to poverty or wealth, adjustment to illness and age.

Claude Wheeler, Prof. St. Peter, Father Vaillant,
Archbishop Latour (and, to a lesser degree, Marian Forrester and Myra Henshawe and the many secondary or
episodic characters in *One of Ours* and the succeeding
books) are thus fully as real as Alexandra, Thea and
Ántonia, their more realistic predecessors. In fact they
are more so; they touch so much more of life.

They may have renounced the world and live in daily
abnegation, daily-renewed consecration of their lives to
an immaterial end, but the beautiful thing about them is
that they never mutilate life.

They love the color and the feel of things, love to finger
the beautiful shapes of natural objects and the beautiful
natural shapes of man-made work of art and tool. They
delight in fine poetry and in music, enjoy good wine and
nicely-gotten food. They never lose their early contact
with the elements. Water, sunshine and earth, while they
renew their strength, keep them free from dryness, im-
patience, and pride. Nor, however superior to the common
run of men (superior in intellect, will power, ideality,
imagination and sensitiveness), do they feel above, or
outside of, humanity—with the simplest, Augustines, Ja-
cintos, and Sadas, they talk and deal on a foot of perfect
equality.

They are the high-water mark of Willa Cather's art,
her most precious legacy to the world, compound, the
best of them, Thea and Claude, Professor and Archbishop,
like Greek Hercules-Apollo, Renaissance Antony, Adonis,
or Adam, or modern Martin Eden or Meredithian hero,

of physical vigor, sensuality, beauty of body, of character and of mind.

They are of course exceptions —exceptions in a world of abortions and failures, dilettantes and plodders, simple trusting souls and mean grasping ones.

Enid, Bayliss, Ivy Peters, one or two episodic characters more, mean grasping men and women are few in Willa Cather's work. Life is too short, and too beautiful, she seems to think, for the artist to spend much of his time criticizing and denouncing when he can be singing the beauty of prairie and of desert, the glory of man's effort, the pathos and greatness of his passions. And so, though she leaves us in no doubt as to what she thinks of the growing cult of mechanization, prohibition, sterilization and xenophobia gradually spreading over America and altering the face of even her beloved West,[3] Willa Cather prefers to sing the simple pains and pleasures and the generous loyalties of simple men; the subtler, more conscious despairs and triumphs of more complex personalities; or to let her imagination play in lands and in ages untainted by the curse of industrial civilization and material prosperity, lands and ages in which men innocent of puritanic inhibitions lived original lives.

Calm, pitiless denunciation of all that tends to standardize or to emasculate men, to enslave them to mechanical rules or, worse still, to mechanical pleasures; impassioned vindication of passion, romantic evasion into the past or the far-away; a strong sense of reality, a strong sense of the importance and the beauty of the thousand little touches that go to the making (and recreating) of landscape or man; a sound valuation of the interdependence of intelligence, moral energy, and physical vigor; an appreciation of the beauty of simple, single-minded human effort (Ántonia's or Thea's) and of wild, untamed nature; as vivid an appreciation of the beauty of culture,

refinement, complexity, and the beauty of a landscape
humanized by suffering or by art—Willa Cather has all
these, and more, her world is a harmonious whole, a well-
balanced world for all its glorification of passion and of
feeling.

Her work is a classical work. Classical, because its in-
nate romanticism is checked by realism and both are made
subservient to an ardent love of life and a respect for
truth. Classical, because the problems she studies are
problems of general and permanent interest. Classical,
because of its style.

"A style with the translucence of sky; a beauty, cool,
grave, persuasive; deep feeling under perfect control."[4]
A style so utterly purged of opaque rhetoric, so unobtrusive and smooth-going, so free from mannerism and
over-emphasis, so intimately welded to the thought or
feeling that, as in Racine's case, whereas no reader can
fail to remark its distinction or be moved by its absence
of cheap emotion, only the analytical mind, only the
reader who reads twice, will notice its infallible choice of
the right epithet and the right word, and its incom-
parable clarity. A truly classical style, expressive in its
restraint,[5] original and yet not eccentric, "old and new,
easily contemporary with all time."[6]

"Valor, candor, tolerance, truthfulness." In these Car-
lyle saw Shakespeare's morality. "No *twisted*, poor con-
vex-concave mirror, reflecting all objects with its own
convexities and concavities; a perfectly *level* mirror."
Such the mirror of Shakespeare's mind and work. Such
also Willa Cather's in her best books.

BIBLIOGRAPHY

A—Books by Willa Cather
B—Prefaces by Willa Cather
C—Willa Cather's contributions to periodicals
D—Articles and Essays on Willa Cather

A

A COMPLETE BIBLIOGRAPHY OF WILLA CATHER'S BOOKS

1. APRIL TWILIGHTS. Boston: R. G. Badger, 1903, 52 pp. Reprinted with additional poems, 1923 (see 10 below).

2. THE TROLL GARDEN. New York: McClure, Philipps and Co., 1905, 253 pp. *Contents:* Flavia and Her Artists, pp. 1-54; The Sculptor's Funeral, pp. 57-84 (Y) (and cf. below C-1905); The Garden Lodge, pp. 87-110; A Death in the Desert, pp. 113-154 (Y) (and cf. below C-1903); The Marriage of Phaedra, pp. 157-192; A Wagner Matinée, pp. 195-210 (Y) (and cf. below C-1904); Paul's Case. A Study in Temperament, pp. 213-253 (Y) (and cf. below C-1905). (Y—reprinted in YOUTH AND THE BRIGHT MEDUSA, see 7 below.)

3. ALEXANDER'S BRIDGE. Boston: Houghton Mifflin Company, 1912, 175 pp. First printed serially (ALEXANDER'S MASQUERADE) in *McClure's Magazine* (see C-1912 below). New edition with Preface by Willa Cather, 1922 (see 8 below).

4. O PIONEERS! Boston: Houghton Mifflin Company, 1913, 309 pp.

5. THE SONG OF THE LARK. Boston: Houghton Mifflin Company, 1915, 490 pp.

6. MY ÁNTONIA. Boston: Houghton Mifflin Company, 1918, 419 pp. New edition, with revised introduction, 1926 (see 13 below).

7. YOUTH AND THE BRIGHT MEDUSA. New York: Alfred A. Knopf, 1920, 303 pp. *Contents:* Coming, Aphrodite! pp. 11-78 (cf. C-1917 below); The Diamond Mine, pp. 79-139 (cf. C-1916); A Gold Slipper, pp. 140-168 (cf. C-1917); Scandal, pp. 169-198 (cf. C-1919); Paul's Case, pp. 199-234 (T. G.); A Wagner Matinée, pp. 235-247 (T. G.); The Sculptor's Funeral, pp. 248-272 (T. G.); A Death in the Desert, pp. 273-303 (T. G.). (T. G.—reprinted from THE TROLL GARDEN, see 2 above.)

8. (See A-3.) ALEXANDER'S BRIDGE. Boston: Houghton Mifflin Company, 1922, iv and 175 pp. New edition, with Preface by Willa Cather, of 3 above.

9. ONE OF OURS. New York: Alfred A. Knopf, 1922, 459 pp.

10. (See 1 above.) APRIL TWILIGHTS AND OTHER POEMS. New York:

Alfred A. Knopf, 1923, 72 pp. New Edition, with twelve additional poems, of 1 above.

11. A Lost Lady. New York: Alfred A. Knopf, 1923, 174 pp. First printed serially in *The Century* (see C-1923 below).

12. The Professor's House. New York: Alfred A. Knopf, 1925, 283 pp. First printed serially in *Collier's* (see C-1925 below).

13. (See 6 above) My Ántonia. Boston: Houghton Mifflin Company, 1926, 419 pp. New edition, with revised introduction, of 6 above.

14. My Mortal Enemy. New York: Alfred A. Knopf, 1926, 120 pp.

15. Death Comes for the Archbishop. New York: Alfred A. Knopf, 1927, 303 pp. First printed serially in *The Forum* (see C-1927 below).

B

Prefaces by Willa Cather

1. Preface to new edition of Alexander's Bridge, 1922 (see 8 above).

2. Introduction to *The Fortunate Mistress*, by Daniel Defoe. New York: Alfred A. Knopf, 1924.

3. *The Best Stories of Sarah Orne Jewett*, selected and arranged with a preface by Willa Cather. Boston: Houghton Mifflin Company, 1925 (2 vols.).

C

A Complete Bibliography of Willa Cather's Contributions to Periodicals
(R-Reprint)

1900 Eric Hermannson's Soul (*Cosmopolitan* 28: 633-44. April). Grandmother, think not . . . —poem (*Critic* 36: 308. April and *Current Literature* 28: 161. May). R. in April Twilights (see A-1 and 10 above) and in *McClure's* and *Current Literature* (see below, 1909).

The Man Who Wrote Narcissus (*Ladies' Home Journal* 17: 11. Nov.).

Asphodel—poem (*Critic* 37; 565. Dec.).

1901 In Media Vita—poem (*Lippincott's Magazine* 67: 623. May). R. in April Twilights (A-1 and 10 above).

El Dorado (*New England Magazine* n.s. 24: 357-69. June).

1902 Namesake—poem (*Lippincott's* 69: 482. April). R. in *McClure's* (below, 1907).

The Professor's Commencement (*New England Magazine* n.s. 26: 481-8. June).

IN ROSE-TIME—poem (*Lippincott's* 70: 97. July).

THE TREASURE OF FAR ISLAND (*New England Magazine* n.s. 27: 234-49. Oct.).

1903   A DEATH IN THE DESERT (*Scribner's* 33: 109-21. Jan.). R. in THE TROLL GARDEN (A-2) and YOUTH . . . (A-7).

1904   A WAGNER MATINÉE (*Everybody's*. March). R. in THE TROLL GARDEN (A-2) and YOUTH . . . (A-7).

1905   THE SCULPTOR'S FUNERAL (*McClure's* 24: 329-6. Jan.). R. in THE TROLL GARDEN (A-2) and YOUTH . . . (A-7).

PAUL'S CASE (*McClure's* 25: 74-83. May). R. from THE TROLL GARDEN (A-2) (published March, 1905). R. in YOUTH . . . (A-10); *Contemporary Short Stories*, edited by K. A. Robinson, Boston: Houghton Mifflin Company, 1924; *The Golden Book Magazine* (see below 1927).

1906   ——

1907   NAMESAKE—poem (*McClure's* 28: 492-7. March). R. from *Lippincott's* (see above 1902).

PROFILE (*McClure's* 29: 135-0. June).

EVENING SONG—poem (*McClure's* 29: 365. Aug.).

THE WILLING MUSE (*Century* 74: 550-7. Aug.).

ELEANOR'S HOUSE (*McClure's* 29: 623-0. Oct.).

AUTUMN MELODY—poem (*McClure's* 30: 106. Nov.). R. in APRIL TWILIGHTS AND OTHER POEMS (A-10).

STAR DIAL—poem (*McClure's* 30: 202. Dec.).

1908   LAMENT FOR MARSYAS—poem (*McClure's* 30: 453. Feb.). R. from APRIL TWILIGHTS (A-1).

PRAIRIE DAWN—poem (*McClure's* 31: 229. June). R. from APRIL TWILIGHTS (A-1).

TAVERN—poem (*McClure's* 31: 419. Aug.).

ON THE GULL'S ROAD (*McClure's* 32: 145-2. Dec.).

1909   FIDES, SPES—poem (*McClure's* 32: 362. Feb.). R. from APRIL TWILIGHTS (A-1).

GRANDMOTHER, THINK NOT . . . —poem (*McClure's* 32: 649, April, and *Current Literature* 47: 106, July). R. from APRIL TWILIGHTS, and already published twice before (see above A-1, C-1900).

THE ENCHANTED BLUFF (*Harper's Monthly Magazine* 118: 774-1. April).

THE PALATINE—poem (*McClure's* 33: 158-9. June). R. in APRIL TWILIGHTS AND OTHER POEMS (A-10).

PROVENCAL LEGEND—poem (*McClure's* 33: 519. Sept.). R. from APRIL TWILIGHTS (A-1).

LONDON ROSES—poem (*McClure's* 34: 61. Nov.). R. from APRIL TWILIGHTS (A-1).

1910   ——

1911   THE POOR MINSTREL—poem (*McClure's* 36: 376. Feb.). R. from APRIL TWILIGHTS (A-1).

THE SWEDISH MOTHER—poem (*McClure's* 37: 541. Sept.). R. in APRIL TWILIGHTS AND OTHER POEMS (A-10).

THE JOY OF NELLY DEANE (*Century* 82: 859-7. Oct.)

1912 ALEXANDER'S MASQUERADE (*McClure's* 38: 384-95, 523-36, 658-68. Feb. to April). R. as ALEXANDER'S BRIDGE (see above A-3).

BEHIND THE SINGER TOWER (*Collier's National Weekly* 49: 16-17. May 18).

SPANISH JOHNNY—poem (*McClure's* 39: 204. June). R. in APRIL TWILIGHTS AND OTHER POEMS (A-10) and in *Literary Digest* (see below 1923).

THE BOHEMIAN GIRL (*McClure's* 39: 420-43. Aug.).

PRAIRIE SPRING—poem (*McClure's* 40: 226. Dec.). R. in O PIONEERS! (A-4) and in APRIL TWILIGHTS AND OTHER POEMS (A-10).

1913 PLAYS OF REAL LIFE (*McClure's* 40: 63-2. March).

TRAINING FOR THE BALLET (*McClure's* 41: 85-95. Oct.).

THREE AMERICAN SINGERS (*McClure's* 42: 33-48. Dec.).

A LIKENESS—poem (*Scribner's* 54: 711-2, Dec. and *Literary Digest* 48: 219. Jan. 1914). R. in APRIL TWILIGHTS AND OTHER POEMS (A-10).

1914 NEW TYPES OF ACTING (*McClure's* 42: 41-51. Feb.).

1915 THE SWEATED DRAMA (*McClure's* 44: 17-28. Jan.).

STREET IN PACKINGTOWN—poem (*Century* 90: 23. May). R. in APRIL TWILIGHTS AND OTHER POEMS (A-10).

CONSEQUENCES (*McClure's* 46: 30-2. Nov.).

1916 THE BOOKKEEPER'S WIFE (*Century* 92: 51-9. May). R. in *The Golden Book Magazine* (see below 1929).

THE DIAMOND MINE (*McClure's* 47: 7-11. Oct.). R. in YOUTH AND THE BRIGHT MEDUSA (A-7).

1917 A GOLD SLIPPER (*Harper's* 134: 166-74. Jan.). R. in YOUTH AND THE BRIGHT MEDUSA (A-7) and in *The Golden Book Magazine* (see below 1926).

1918 ARDESSA (*Century* 96: 105-116. May).

1919 SCANDAL (*Century* 98: 433-45. Aug.). R. in YOUTH AND THE BRIGHT MEDUSA (A-7).

1920 ON THE ART OF FICTION (*The Borzoi* 1920).

1921 ——

1922 NOVEL DÉMEUBLÉ (*New Republic* 30: sup. 5-6. April 12). R. in *Modern Essays*, edited by Christopher Morley, New York: Harcourt, Brace & Co., 1924).

1923 A LOST LADY (*Century* 105: 803-22, 106; 75-94, 289-309, April to June). R. in book form (see above A-11).

SPANISH JOHNNY—poem (*Literary Digest* 78: 34. July). R. from *McClure's* (see above 1912) and APRIL TWILIGHTS AND OTHER POEMS (A-10).

NEBRASKA: THE END OF THE FIRST CYCLE (*Nation* 117: 236-8. Sept. 5). R. in *These United States*, edited by E. H. Gruening. New York: Boni and Liveright, 1923.

1924 ——

1925 UNCLE VALENTINE (*Woman's Home Companion* 52: 7-9, Feb. 15-16, March).
THE PROFESSOR'S HOUSE (*Collier's* 75: 5-7, etc., 76: 30-35, etc., June 6-Aug. 1.). R. in book form (see above A-12).
KATHERINE MANSFIELD (*The Borzoi* 1925).

1926 A GOLD SLIPPER (*The Golden Book Magazine* 3: 359-6. March). R. from *Harper's* (see above 1917) and YOUTH . . . (A-7).
COMING, APHRODITE! (*The Golden Book Magazine* 4: 591-609. Nov.). R. from YOUTH . . . (A-7).

1927 DEATH COMES FOR THE ARCHBISHOP (*Forum* 77: 22-9, 286-97, 450-61, 612-25, 770-84, 930-42. Jan. to June). R. in book form (see above A-15).
PAUL'S CASE (*The Golden Book Magazine* 5: 681-0. May). R. from *McClure's* THE TROLL GARDEN, YOUTH . . . and *Contemporary Short Stories* (see above 1905).

1928 ————

1929 DOUBLE BIRTHDAY (*Forum* 81: 78-82. Feb.).
THE BOOKKEEPER'S WIFE (*The Golden Book Magazine* 10: 74-8, Nov.). R. from *The Century* (see above 1916).

1930 NEIGHBOR ROSICKY (*Woman's Home Companion* 57: 7-9 April; 13-14 May).

D

ARTICLES AND ESSAYS ON WILLA CATHER
(Alphabetically arranged)

N.B.—The list does not aim at completeness. In particular it does not include mere book reviews.

Anonymous."Willa Cather—A Biographical Sketch. An English Opinion" (being a reprint of Alexander Porterfield's article, q.v.). "An American Opinion" (being a reprint of an American review of DEATH COMES . . .). "A Letter from Willa Cather" (her letter to *The Commonweal*, cf. above, p. 81), and "An Abridged Bibliography." New York: Alfred A. Knopf, Publisher. (Referred to in the course of this book as "Knopf pamphlet.")

———— Article in *The National Cyclopedia of Biography*. New York: James T. White Co. (Contemporary Vol. A, p. 537).

Bartlett, Alice A. "Dynamics of American Poetry" (Emily Dickinson, Willa Cather, Robert Hillyer). *Poetry Review*, London, 16 (1925): 405-414.

Carroll, Latrobe. *The Bookman* 53: 212-6. May, 1921.

Dickinson, A. D. *Best Books of Our Time* Garden City, N. Y.: Doubleday, Doran & Co., 1928.

Michaud, Régis. *The American Novel To-day*, A Sociological and Psychological Study. Boston: Little, Brown and Co., 1928.

Morris, Lloyd. *North American Review* 219: 641-52. May, 1924.

Moss, David. Bibliographical check list. *Publishers' Weekly*, 1923, 103: 23 (corrections and additions do. 1769-0 and 104: 1453).

Overton, Grant M. *The Women Who Make Our Novels* (pp. 256-1, dated 1915). New York: Moffat, Yard and Co., 1918.

Porterfield, Alexander. *The London Mercury* 13: 516-24, March, 1926. Reprinted in *Contemporary American Authors*, Papers from *The London Mercury*, ed. J. C. Squire. New York: Henry Holt & Co., 1928. Also in "Knopf pamphlet" (see above).

Rascoe, Burton. "Contemporary Reminiscences." *Arts and Decoration* 20: 28, April, 1924.

Sergeant, Elizabeth Shipley. *Fire Under the Andes:* A Group of North American Portraits. New York: Alfred A. Knopf, 1927. Reprinted from *The New Republic* 43: 91-4, June 17, 1925.

Sherman, Stuart. *Critical Woodcuts* (pp. 32-48). New York & London: Charles Scribner's Sons, 1926. Essay entitled "Willa Cather and the Changing World."

Tittle, W. "Glimpses of Interesting Americans." *The Century* 110: 309-3, July, 1925.

Van Doren, Carl. *Contemporary American Novelists*. New York: The Macmillan Co., 1922. Reprinted from *The Nation* 113: 92-3, July, 1921.

West, Rebecca. *The Strange Necessity*. Garden City, N. Y.: Doubleday, Doran & Co., 1928. Essay entitled "The Classic Artist."

Whipple, T. K. *Spokesmen*, Modern Writers and American Life (pp. 139-160). New York & London: D. Appleton and Co., 1928. Reprinted from *The Literary Review* 4: 331-2, Dec. 8, 1923.

NOTES

I

(1) *My Ántonia*, 156.

II

(1) The following quotation is a connected transcription of information given by Willa Cather in three different places: the G. M. Overton and L. Carroll interviews (see bibliography of articles and essays on Willa Cather, p. 103 of this book) and the short biographical sketch forming pp. 1-3 of the "Knopf pamphlet" (see *do.*). The italics and the notes are mine.

(2) This information I find in G. M. Overton.

(3) Readers of *My Ántonia* will notice the close parallel between Jim Burden's experience in that book and Willa Cather's as a child.

(4) "If a sparrow comes before my window I take part in its existence and pick about the gravel."—"A poet is the most unpoetical of anything in existence, because he has no Identity—he is continually in for and filling some other body." KEATS's *Letters*.

(5) "La mémoire, l'organe intellectuel le plus utile à l'artiste." PROUST on Ruskin (*Pastiches et Mélanges*, p. 144 n.) ——"Memory, according to Greek legend, was the mother of the Muses." MURRAY, *Euripides*, p. 106.

(6) "Wagner says, in his most beautiful opera, that art is only a way of remembering youth. And the older we grow the more precious it seems to us, and the more richly we can present that memory. When we've got it all out—the last, the finest thrill of it, the brightest hope of it . . . then we stop. We do nothing but repeat after that. The stream has reached the level of its source. That's our measure." (*The Song of the Lark*, p. 460.)

(7) "It's a queer thing about the flat country—it takes hold of you, or it leaves you perfectly cold. A great many people find it dull and monotonous; they like a church steeple, an old mill, a waterfall, country all touched up and furnished, like a German Christmas card. I go everywhere, I admire all kinds of country. I tried to live in France. But when I strike the open plains, something happens. I'm home, I breathe differently. [Cf. similar feeling in 'Going Home (Burlington Route),' *April Twilights and Other Poems*]. That love of great spaces, of rolling open country like the sea—it's the grand passion of my life. I tried for years to get over it. I've stopped trying. It's incurable."—Willa Cather in "Knopf pamphlet," p. 3.

(8) "Knopf pamphlet," p. 2—Willa Cather entered college in 1891

and received her B. A. degree in 1895. (Information kindly communicated by the Registrar of the University of Nebraska.)

(9) Willa Cather in the L. CARROLL interview.

(10) "It is always hard to write about the things that are near your heart. From a kind of instinct of self-protection you distort and disguise them."—Willa Cather in G. M. OVERTON.

(11) Willa Cather in G. M. OVERTON.

(12) "As I got toward my senior year, I began to admire, for the first time, writing for writing's sake . . . Henry James . . . for me, he was the perfect writer."—Willa Cather in L. CARROLL, *l.c.*

(13) See below, p. 20.

(14) "One of the few really helpful words I ever heard from an older writer I had from Sarah Orne Jewett when she said to me: 'Of course, one day you will write about your own country. In the meantime get all you can. One must know the world *so well* before one can know the parish.'" (Willa Cather's 1922 preface to *Alexander's Bridge*.)

(15) Cf. above, p. 10, n.7.

(16) See especially *A Lost Lady* (cf. p. 70 below) and, for a strong picture (and strong criticism) of the new order triumphant, *One of Ours* (cf. 97 below).

(17) After she graduated Willa Cather went to Pittsburgh where she had friends and worked there first as telegraph editor and dramatic critic of the Leader, then as head of the English department in the Allegheny High School. Thus the sources (OVERTON and CARROLL) I have used. Willa Cather herself however writes to me: "I had for several years a nominal connection with the Pittsburgh *Leader* but during that time I was in Pittsburgh very little—I was in Colorado and Wyoming for most of every year and was interested in things very different from editorial work." Cf. "Knopf pamphlet," pp. 2-3: "Every summer she went back to Nebraska and Colorado and Wyoming . . . Wherever she went, whatever ties she formed, she always went back to the plains country. The first year she spent in Europe she nearly died of homesickness for it."

(18) In the six years between *The Troll Garden* and *Alexander's Bridge* her only publications were twenty contributions to the magazines, fourteen of which were short poems. (See bibliography B, pp. 100–101.

III

(1) All dates in this section are dates, not of composition, but of first publication.

(2) The only story in which Willa Cather allows her imagination to take her back to the West is *A Death in the Desert. The Sculptor's Funeral* is supposed to take place in Kansas but has no local color. The reference to Nebraska in *A Wagner Matinée* is only used for the sake of contrast and is brief and disparaging.

(3) Or the later *The Diamond Mine, A Gold Slipper* and *Scandal.* Cf. below, pp. 52–54.

(4) Though apparently not to Willa Cather's, as she has not reprinted the story in *Youth and the Bright Medusa* (1920) which includes all the other *Troll Garden* stories except *The Garden Lodge* and *The Marriage of Phaedra.*

(5) Rosamond's husband is neither calm nor unassuming. Like Capt. Forrester and Oswald Henshawe, however, he represents the more human, generous and, in spite of appearances, the more stable half of the couple.

(6) It is preëminently the case in *A Lost Lady.*

(7) 1922 preface to *Alexander's Bridge*, p. viii.

(8) Lloyd MORRIS, Contrast OVERTON's absurd eulogy of the Conventional end of *Alexander's Bridge.*

(9) Stuart SHERMAN's.

(10) Parallel cases would be Dr. Archie's (*The Song of the Lark*), Professor St. Peter's (*The Professor's House*), Marian Forrester's (*A Lost Lady*).

(11) PROUST on Ruskin (*Pastiches et Mélanges*, p. 118).

IV

(1) "It is not always easy for the inexperienced writer to distinguish between his own material and that which he would like to make his own. . . . The things he knows best he takes for granted, since he is not continually thrilled by new discoveries about them. They lie at the bottom of his consciousness, whether he is aware of it or no, and they continue to feed him, but they do not stimulate him" (Willa Cather, 1922 preface to *Alexander's Bridge*).

(2) "I think usually the young writer must have his affair with the external material he covets; must imitate and strive to follow the masters he most admires, until he finds he is starving for reality and cannot make this go any longer. Then he learns that it is not the adventure he sought, but the adventure that sought him, which has made the enduring mark upon him." (*do.*)

(3) Willa Cather in L. CARROLL,—Cf. the parallel passage in Overton: "I had the good fortune to meet Sarah Orne Jewett, who had read all of my early stories [and saw] where my work fell short. She said: 'Write it as it is, don't try to make it like this or that. . . . You'll have to make a way of your own. If the way happens to be new, don't let that frighten you. Don't try to write the kind of short story that this or that magazine wants; write the truth. . . .' I dedicated *O Pioneers* to her because I had talked over some of the characters with her, and . . . I tried to tell the story of the people as truthfully and simply as if I were telling it to her by word of mouth"—As to Sarah Orne Jewett's influence on Willa Cather cf. also above, p. 121 n. 14., and, below, p. 99 (See B-3).

(4) 1922 preface to *Alexander's Bridge.*

(5) Emil is a malcontent like Claude Wheeler, a man at odds with the world and with himself. Compared to Claude, however, he is more violent and less *nuancé.*

(6) Simplicity of soul, accompanied or not with imbecility, holds

a fascination over certain artists (Wordsworth, Conrad, Ramuz, Willa Cather herself: cf. besides Ivar, Old Mahailey (*One of Ours*), Augusta (*The Professor's House*), Russian Peter (*My Ántonia*), etc.). These artists often seem to wonder whether it does not express supreme, or at least a superior, wisdom.

(7) "Marie was incapable of being lukewarm about everything that pleased her. She simply didn't know how to give a half-hearted response" (217).

(8) "There was about Alexandra something of the impervious calm of the fatalist, always disconcerting to very young people, who cannot feel that the heart lives at all unless it is still at the mercy of storms; unless its strings can scream to the touch of pain" (226).

(9) Willa Cather in L. CARROLL.

(10) Cf. later, pp. 49-51 (footnotes).

(11) *O Pioneers*, 204-205.

V

(1) Cf. in particular Spanish Johnny, Old Wunsch and Harsanyi in this book, Gerhardt in *One of Ours*, etc.

(2) Cf. later, pp. 52-54.

(3) One is inevitably reminded here of Thomas Hardy and Edmond Gosse, both given up for dead at their birth.

(4) Cf. later, p. 58n.

(5) "But it is necessary to know if you know somethings. Somethings cannot be taught. If you not know in the beginning, you not know in the end. For a singer there must be something in the inside from the beginning. . . . Yes, when you are barely six, you must know that already. That is the beginning of all things; *der Geist, die Phantasie*. It must be in the baby, when it makes its first cry, like *der Rhythmus*, or it is not to be. . . . Oh, much you can learn! *Aber nicht die Americanischen Fräulein*. They have nothing inside them. . . . They are like the ones in the *Märchen*, a grinning face and hollow in the insides. Something they can learn, oh, yes, may-be! But the secret—what make the rose to red, the sky to blue, the man to love—*in der Brust, in der Brust* it is, *und ohne dieses giebt es keine Kunst, giebt es keine Kunst!*" (78).

(6) Cf. also p. 87: "In his tastes too the doctor was romantic. Though he read Balzac all the year through, he still enjoyed the Waverley Novels as much as when he had first come upon them . . . in his grandfather's library. . . . He liked Scott's women. . . ."

(7) WHIPPLE, *Spokesmen*, 150.

(8) A similar tendency can be found in some male writers, in a converse form. Dickens's and Scott's heroines are classical examples.

(9) The whole passage (474 ff.) should be quoted.

(10) The strongest expression of this feeling in *The Song of the Lark* is perhaps to be found in this passage (pp. 198-9):

"She was not ready to listen until the second number, Dvorak's Symphony in E minor, called on the programme,

'From the New World.' The first theme had scarcely been given out when her mind became clear; instant composure fell upon her, and with it came the power of concentration. This was music she could understand, music from the New World indeed! Strange how, as the first movement went on, it brought back to her that high table-land above Laramie; the grass-grown wagon trails, the far-away peaks of the snowy range, the wind and the eagles, that old man and the first telegraph message.

"When the first movement ended, Thea's hands and feet were cold as ice. She was too much excited to know anything except that she wanted something desperately, and when the English horns gave out the theme of the Largo, she knew that what she wanted was exactly that. Here were the sand-hills, the grasshoppers and locusts, all the things that wakened and chirped in the early morning; the reaching and reaching of high plains, the immeasurable yearning of all flat lands. There was home in it, too; first memories, first mornings long ago; the amazement of a new soul in a new world; a soul new and yet old, that had dreamed something despairing, something glorious, in the dark before it was born; a soul obsessed by what it did not know, under the cloud of a past it could not recall."

(11) Alexandra, Ántonia, Eden Bowen (*Coming Aphrodite!*), Cressida Garnet, (*The Diamond Mine*), Claude Wheeler, Prof. St. Peter, would all be cases to the point.

(12) Is not doggedness the most typical quality of the men and women of her race?

(13) As Thea is about to make her *début* in a Wagner opera at Dresden, Dr. Archie writes asking Thea to come back if she wants to see her mother once more. Thea, knowing herself at the eve of her first decisive battle, lets her mother die without having seen her again.

(14) This is early examplified in her fondness for "Spanish Johnny" and other decidedly low-class Mexicans.

VI

(1) The first part of *My Ántonia* indeed resembles a series of etchings illustrating pioneer Nebraska. They could easily be given titles: *Black Hawk, Night; Immigrants' Arrival; the Basement Kitchen; Garden in the Prairie; The Rattlesnake; Russian Settlers; Ántonia; Breaking Sod;* etc.

(2) That sentimentality is not entirely absent from *O Pioneers*, see convincing proof in Prof. WHIPPLE, 149. A severe judge might also consider Alexandra's marriage to Carl Lindstrum like Thea's marriage (and for similar reasons) a concession to sentimentalists —or to the sentimentalist in the author.

(3) And not only her heroine but the actual Ántonia as well, for

as Willa Cather herself has confessed, Ántonia "was a Bohemian girl who was good to me when I was a child . . . from the time I was eight until I was twelve. She was big-hearted and essentially romantic." (CARROLL.)

(4) If anybody should wonder how what was beneficial to *O Pioneers* could be harmful to *My Ántonia*, I should point to what I say at the beginning of the next paragraph, and add that even in *O Pioneers*, as witness its imperfection of structure, realism was not wholly beneficial.

I think it only fair to add that Lloyd MORRIS with whom I am generally in agreement praises in his criticism of *My Ántonia* Willa Cather's growing sense of reality and "advancing capacity for imaginative recasting of its elements!"

(5) Stuart SHERMAN, *Critical Woodcuts*, p. 43.

(6) May I submit a third, complementary hypothesis as to the cause of *My Ántonia's* structural weakness? With Ántonia, we said, the book stands and falls—was she not too simple a personality to fill a whole novel? Should not Willa Cather rather have made her the heroine of a short story (the length of, say, *The Diamond Mine*)? Once you look at it in this way do not the weak parts of *My Ántonia* (Books II and III in particular) look suspiciously like padding (unconscious padding of course)?

VII

(1) In the series, if not in Willa Cather's work (he has several traits in common with Claude Wheeler).

(2) *A Gold Slipper* (*Youth and the Bright Medusa*, pp. 159-60).

(3) *Do., do.*, p. 162.

VIII

(1) *The Song of the Lark, One of Ours, The Professor's House,* and *Death* . . . are, to my mind, her 'big four.'

(2) Claude Wheeler is of course only a *comparatively* complex figure—complex in comparison with Ántonia, Alexandra or Thea, not with Prof. St. Peter. His problem is also in part Emil Bergson's in *O Pioneers*, but Emil's adjustment to life is but a side interest in *O Pioneers*, not the central problem Claude Wheeler's is in *One of Ours*.

(3) The few exceptions are passing remarks like these: "Evidently, it took more intelligence to spend money than to make it" (86); "this war has taught us all how little the made things matter. Only the feeling matters" (315); "But as for me, I never knew there was anything worth living for, till this war came on. Before that, the world seemed like a business proposition" (340).

(4) H. M. TOMLINSON on *Sergeant Grischa, The Saturday Review of Literature*, Vol. V, No. 27, Jan. 26, 1929.

(5) "What I always want to do," Willa Cather said at the time she was writing *One of Ours*, "is to make the writing count for

less and less and the people for more. In this new novel I'm trying to cut out all analysis, observation, description, even the, picture-making quality, in order to make things and people tell their own story simply by juxtaposition, without any persuasion or explanation on my part. . . . Mere cleverness must go. I'd like the writing to be so lost in the object that it doesn't exist for the reader— except for the reader who knows how difficult it is to lose writing in the object." (Willa Cather in L. CARROLL.)

To see how completely she realized her intentions compare the racy, colloquial dialogue in *One of Ours* with the 'literary dialogue' (that reproduced on p. 53 above for example) of even a comparatively late work like *A Gold Slipper* (1917).

As to Willa Cather's felicitous use of action to express character see, e.g., the striking incident of Mr. Wheeler cutting the loaded cherry tree to—save his wife's back. A good example of brevity of trait is this four line sketch: "The Colonel was not a very martial figure; short, fat, with slouching shoulders, and a lumpy back like a sack of potatoes. Though he wasn't much over forty, he was bald, *and his collar would easily slip over his head without being unbuttoned*" (281). There are many such sketches. The hero himself is described in less than twenty lines at the beginning of the book, then we have no more portraits of him except for one or two occasions on which he is arrested in a position of suspended action.

(6) For a typical example of this impartiality of hers we must take her portrait of Mr. Wheeler, Claude's father. After impressing on us, in a few well-selected traits, the massive personality and heavy jocularity of the man, Willa Cather paints his moral por trait in such short touches as these: "He had magnificent health, and illness in himself or in other people struck him as humorous. . . . There was this to be said for Nat Wheeler, that he liked every sort of human creature; he liked good people and honest people, and he liked rascals and hypocrites almost to the point of loving them. If he heard that a neighbor had played a sharp trick or done something particularly mean, he was sure to drive over to see the man at once, as if he hadn't hitherto appreciated him . . . (etc.)" (8-9).

(7) Cf. also p. 42: "Young men went into the ministry because they were timid or lazy and wanted society to take care of them; because they wanted to be pampered by kind, trusting women like his mother." In Mr. Kronborg and Mr. Larsen (*The Song of the Lark*) Willa Cather had already painted two such preachers. Her sketch of Edward Chapin, Claude's lodger in Frankfort, is also quite in the Lewisian manner. "Chapin had been going to the Temple College for four years, and it would probably take him two years more to complete the course. . . . His natural stupidity must have been something quite out of the ordinary; after years of reverential study, he could not read the Greek Testament without a lexicon and grammar at his elbow. . . ." (27-28).

(8) P. 21.—"His mother was old-fashioned. . . . According to

her conception of education, one should learn, not think; and above all one must not enquire" (22).

(9) "Everything about a man's embrace was distasteful to Enid; something inflicted upon women, like the pain of childbirth—for Eve's transgression, perhaps" (172).

(10) Claude becomes engaged in July 1914. He marries in June 1915.

(11) Claude finds France very different from what he had imagined it to be. His representation of it, in fact, was in its way as naïve as his men's representation of Paris. "Only a little way up that river was Paris. . . . The Seine, they felt sure, must be very much wider there, and it was spanned by many bridges, all longer than the bridge over the Missouri at Omaha. There would be spires and golden domes past counting, all the buildings higher than anything in Chicago, and brilliant—dazzlingly brilliant, nothing grey and shabby about it like this old Rouen. They attributed to the city of their desire incalculable immensity, bewildering vastness, Babylonian hugeness and heaviness—the only attributes they had been taught to admire" (279).

IX

(1) Nothing shows the perfection of Willa Cather's art in this book better than the opening scene where Ivy Peters, then a boy of eighteen or nineteen, slits a woodpecker's eyes and coolly leaves the bird to its misery. The scene is brief and hard to forget.

(2) One might criticize the (comparatively) happy ending of the book, saying that after Mrs. Forrester became Ivy Peters' mistress and was cast off by him she could only end in worse degradation and misery. The objection, however, would not be quite fair. True, Willa Cather has shunned bringing Mrs. Forrester still lower down, but her ruin is complete enough for poetic justice to be satisfied, and her last bizzare marriage shows only too clearly how much stronger her thirst to live was than her sense of honor, and how utterly unbalanced, how utterly "lost," she has become since Captain Forrester's death.

(3) I cannot therefore agree with such uncritical statements as Alexander PORTERFIELD's "good as *One of Ours* is, *A Lost Lady* is supremely better," or "Miss Cather's next book [*A Lost Lady*] is by common consent her best—a masterpiece." To give *A Lost Lady* such absolute praise it is necessary to forget the difference in scale and treatment between it and Willa Cather's full-length (and full-strength) novels.

(4) Alexander PORTERFIELD.

X

(1) Utterly gone now the photographic truth of *My Ántonia* and the earlier books.

(2) "Canadian French on one side, and American farmers on the other" (12).

(3) Prof. St. Peter and a few of his colleagues "resisted the new commercialism, the aim to 'show results' that was undermining and vulgarizing education. The state legislature and the board of regents seemed determined to make a trade school of the university. Candidates for the degree of bachelor of arts were allowed credits for commercial studies; courses in bookkeeping, experimental farming, domestic science, dressmaking and what not. Every year the regents tried to diminish the number of credits required in science and the humanities. The liberal appropriations, the promotions and increases in salary, all went to the professors who worked with the regents to abolish the purely cultural studies. Out of a faculty of sixty, there were perhaps twenty men who made any serious stand for scholarship . . ." (140).

(4) Kathleen's portrait is built of such revealing little touches as this: "When she was a student at the university, he (her father) used sometimes to see her crossing the campus alone, her head and shoulders lowered against the wind, her muff beside her face, her narrow skirt clinging close. There was something too plucky, too 'I can-go-it-alone,' about her quick step and jaunty little head; he didn't like it, it gave him a sudden pang. He would always call to her and catch up with her and make her take his arm and be docile" (64).

(5) Of this impartiality of Willa Cather's, of her infallible felicity in selecting the characteristic trait passages like the following are convincing proofs: "Crane was wearing a grey cotton coat, shrunk to a rag by washing, though he wasn't working with fluids or batteries to-night, but at a roll-top desk littered with papers. The room was like any study behind a lecture room; dusty books, dusty files, but no apparatus—except a spirit-lamp and a little saucepan in which the physicist heated water for his cocoa at regular intervals. He was working by the glare of an unshaded electric bulb of high power—the man seemed to have no feeling for comfort of any kind. . . . St. Peter watched him scribbling with his fountain pen. The hands that were so deft in delicate manipulations were white and soft-looking; the fingers long and loosely hung, stained with chemicals, and blunted at the tips like a violinist's. His head was square, and the lower part of his face was covered by a reddish, matted beard. His pale eyes and fawn-colored eyebrows were outbalanced by his mouth, his most conspicuous feature. One always remembered about Crane that unexpected, startling red mouth in a setting of kinky beard. The lips had no modelling, they were as thick at the corners as in the middle, and he spoke through them rather than with them. He seemed painfully conscious of them" (144-5).

(6) One of the best I know anywhere. It tells you much without seeming to do anything but follow the professor's casual steps through the deserted house, and, from the very first lines the right

note is struck, the passage of time made apparent, the reminiscent mood ushered in.

(7) Percy Lubbock, *The Craft of Fiction*, 40.

(8) Stuart Sherman.

XI

(1) Lee Wilson Dodd's review of *My Mortal Enemy, Saturday Review of Literature*, 23-10-26.

(2) *My Mortal Enemy* is Willa Cather's shortest novel. It is only 19,000 words as compared to *A Lost Lady's* 40,000. *The Professor's House* has 70,000, *Death . . .* 75,000. Brevity, often the soul of wit, here spells sketchiness and failure to create.

(3) The narrator, a young girl, is absolutely without character and her interposed presence adds nothing to the story. The other characters, except for Myra's husband, are only episodic, and Myra's husband, as the husband of such a wife would naturally be, is of too retiring and laconic nature to have anything much to say or to do.

XII

(1) Willa Cather's titles are not always very happy. If such titles as *The Troll Garden, The Song of the Lark, Youth and the Bright Medusa*, or *My Mortal Enemy* cannot be called misleading, they fail however in that they are too vague; they have too remote a connection with the books they introduce.

(2) In a letter addressed to *The Commonweal*. The letter is dated Nov. 23, 1927. It has been reprinted in the "Knopf pamphlet" (see bibliography, p. 103).

(3) "Knopf pamphlet," p. 17.

(4) "No one in Cincinnati could tell him (the new bishop) how to get to New Mexico—no one had ever been there. . . . New Mexico lay in the middle of a dark continent. The Ohio merchants knew of two routes only. One was the Santa Fé from St. Louis, but at that time it was dangerous because of Comanche Indian raids. His friends advised Father Latour to go down the river to New Orleans, thence by boat to Galveston, across Texas to San Antonio, and to wind up into New Mexico along the Rio Grande valley. This he had done, but with what misadventures!" (18).

(5) "Knopf pamphlet," p. 19.

(6) The *Legend of Friar Baltazar* (pp. 105-117), the gourmand tyrant of Acoma, the portrait of Father Martinez, the rebellious priest of Taos, have the humorous sensuality and the high color of Fielding's portrait of Parson Trulliber or Daudet's Curé de Cucugnan or Père Gaucher.

(7) How exact, precise, and perfectly assimilated Willa Cather's knowledge of Catholic usage, can be seen in such passages as the Prologue, the account of Father Joseph's reception by the Pope

(231), the reference on p. 286 to the "College for Foreign Missions in the rue du Bac," etc., etc.

(8) Cf. quotation above, p. 81.

(9) The suggestion of "something reptilian" about the Indians is increased by the mysterious mountain cavern episode ("The Stone Lip") with its implications of serpent worship and human sacrifice to snakes.

(10) To give only one proof of it cf. his delicate appreciation of the human quality in things of every day use—as, e.g., the pleasant irregularity of "the thick clay walls" of his study, "finished on the inside by the deft palms of Indian women" (32).

(11) Cf., e.g.: "His bowed head was not that of an ordinary man—it was built for the seat of a fine intelligence. His brow was open, generous, reflective, his features handsome and somewhat severe. . . . His manners, even when he was alone in the desert, were distinguished. He had a kind of courtesy toward himself, toward his beasts, toward the juniper tree before which he knelt, and the God whom he was addressing . . ." (16).

XIII

(1) I think Willa Cather was right when she made her realists women. Women seem to know earlier than men the extent and the limits of their strength and what they will live for. Possibly, also, when she made her Emils and Carls and Claudes, Willa Cather felt freer to give them of her own doubts and disquietudes than she did when she painted those early heroines who (far different from the later Marian Forrester and Myra Henshawe) are so obviously simplified figures of herself (herself with the unrest and the genius left out).

(2) She had not done so since the days of *The Troll Garden*.

(3) See especially *Youth and the Bright Medusa, One of Ours, A Lost Lady* (cf. above, passim, e.g. 53 and 70). Professor Whipple is thus undoubtedly right in upholding against Carl Van Doren that Willa Cather's "scarification of (her environment), repeated again and again, is as vitriolic as that of any contemporary" (see the whole passage, WHIPPLE, 155).

(4) Stuart SHERMAN, 33.

(5) "Le classicisme . . . , c'est l'art d'exprimer le plus en disant le moins" ANDRÉ GIDE, *Morceaux Choisis*, (85).

(6) SAINTE-BEUVE's essay *"What Is a Classic?"* (1850) (*Causeries du Lundi,* III), (English translation—"Essays by SAINTE-BEUVE. Translated, with an introduction, by Elizabeth Lee. London: Walter Scott, Ltd."—no date).